How to End the Reading War and Serve the Literacy Needs of All Students

D1522087

How to End the Reading War and Serve the Literacy Needs of All Students

A Primer for Parents, Policy Makers, and People Who Care

P. L. Thomas

Furman University

INFORMATION AGE PUBLISHING, INC.
Charlotte, NC • www.infoagepub.com

Library of Congress Cataloging-in-Publication Data

A CIP record for this book is available from the Library of Congress
http://www.loc.gov

ISBN: 978-1-64802-140-4 (Paperback)
      978-1-64802-141-1 (Hardcover)
      978-1-64802-142-8 (E-Book)

Printed in the United States of America

Dedicated to

Renita (Nita) Schmidt, friend, colleague, literacy expert

Skylar and Brees, grandchildren

Contents

INTRODUCTION

Parent Advocacy and the New (but Still Misguided) Phonics Assault on Reading

Many are familiar with various versions of George Santayana's quote, "Those who cannot remember the past are condemned to repeat it," included in a slightly paraphrased form toward the end of Kurt Vonnegut's (1976) *Slapstick*. In response, the novel's narrator adds: "History is merely a list of surprises . . . It can only prepare us to be surprised yet again" (p. 255).

Vonnegut's satirical exchange is fairly bleak and pessimistic, suggesting that we humans are destined to ignore history, destined to make the same mistakes over and over. As an educator for almost 40 years, I have literally lived a significant part of the history of high-stakes accountability in public education. When I started teaching public high school in 1984, South Carolina had just adopted education legislation implementing state standards and high-stakes tests, including exit exams students had to pass to receive a diploma. All of this was being repeated across the United States because of the release of *A Nation at Risk* under Ronald Reagan—a misleading declaration that public schools were failing.

How to End the Reading War and Serve the Literacy Needs of All Students, pages xi–xx
Copyright © 2020 by Information Age Publishing
All rights of reproduction in any form reserved.

Since the early 1980s and throughout the 1990s, states increasingly adopted prescriptive standards for reading and writing as well as math. Schools, teachers, and students have been held accountable for those literacy and math standards through test scores also. This means that the what and how of teaching reading in the United States has been *significantly mandated by state policies* along with state-adopted textbooks and programs that are aligned with those standards and tests.

But I have also spent a great deal of my doctoral work and scholarship examining the history of education, specifically literacy education—how we teach reading and writing—since the early 20th century. One of the most important guiding figures for me about that history of literacy education is Lou LaBrant, the focus of my dissertation.

LaBrant, in her memoir written at age 100, made an important and somewhat angry observation: "'I do not...have much sympathy for those who preach about going 'back to basics.'...'Going back' is impossible and unnecessary'" (as quoted in Thomas, 2001, p. 8). Here, LaBrant is directly confronting the "back to basics" movement occurring under President Reagan while also acknowledging that she had lived and worked through three or four such movements in the United States—fruitlessly repeating a history people failed to learn (think about Santayana and Vonnegut above).

Too often, I feel LaBrant's frustration, and I worry that I am trapped in a real-life *Groundhog Day* (the film made famous with Bill Murray). That is where I currently reside as I offer this book about another reading war in full pitch throughout 2019 in the United States. For this book, I am purposefully using the singular "war" since my case is that the war I am confronting now is different only in minor ways from all the versions of the reading war that have come before every few decades. The reading war is never-ending, it seems, but surprising some of us (mostly journalists, the public, and politicians) nonetheless.

Briefly here in the Introduction, whether you have come to this book because of the current reading war or have not yet waded into that battle—often waged on social media—I want to introduce some of the key positions and issues before working our way to ending that war so that public education can better serve all students' literacy needs.

Fighting the Reading War Again for the First Time

In the chapters to follow, I will explore in detail the reading war occurring in the 1940s and 1990s (Chapter 1) as well as the current reading war

(Chapter 2). But here, I can offer a brief overview of what is common among the perpetual reading war as it relates to teaching reading in U.S. schools.

The reading war may be better called the Phonics War since each round of this fight about teaching reading becomes centered on the place of systematic-intensive phonics instruction. On one side, advocates for systematic-intensive phonics tend to argue that *all* students need is systematic instruction in order to read. These phonics advocates also view reading as a simple process that is grounded in students pronouncing words in order to comprehend. This simple view of reading is mechanical and sequential; their argument is discrete pronunciation of phonemes (smallest units of sound), and words must occur before comprehension.

Differing from this view of the importance of systematic-intensive phonics as well as how humans read is the position that is often associated with two different guiding philosophies of reading instruction, whole language and balanced literacy (both of which will be explained more fully in Chapter 3). This argument for a more complex and idiosyncratic view of teaching reading and reading itself acknowledges that individual students learn to read in a wide variety of ways that cannot be easily prescribed or even described. Some students need less systematic intensive phonics instruction (maybe even none) while others need much more. This position also recognizes that reading is not letter by letter, phoneme by phoneme, or even word by word, but contextual (and chaotic as eye movement research shows).

While advocates for systematic-intensive phonics emphasize decoding (pronouncing) words, others emphasize comprehension and critical literacy, recognizing that students coming to be *independent* and *eager* readers is not a structured or predictable path. Important to note about the distinction is one of the most misleading aspects of the war itself; often the battle is framed as *those for phonics instruction* versus *those against phonics instruction.* More accurately, the war is about the proper place for and the amount of systematic intensive phonics for *all* students.

As I will highlight in Chapter 2, the current reading war has many of the elements noted above, but this new round has adopted the "science of reading" as the marker for systematic intensive phonics and advocates for dyslexic students have added a unique but powerful boost to the call for systematic intensive phonics.

As LaBrant (1949) would argue, I find these two opposing positions have one troubling aspect in common—the overreliance on reading programs that tend to fail students regardless of which side of the war the program fulfills. Teachers are often held accountable for *implementing the reading program,* which becomes a distraction from what students need to become independent, critical, and eager readers. Another key aspect of the current reading war, unlike some of the versions in the past, is that we must acknowledge the point I made above; reading philosophies and how teachers of reading are taught to teach reading and to view the act of reading all mean very little under the weight of standards and high-stakes tests, both of which significantly dictate how students are taught to read and which reading programs teachers must implement in their classes.

Let's consider next, then, the role of parents as advocates for how children are taught to read in formal schools.

Parent Advocacy and the New (but Still Misguided) Phonics Assault on Reading

"School days were eagerly anticipated by Francie," a central character in Betty Smith's (1947) *A Tree Grows in Brooklyn* (p. 143). The novel often is a powerful fictional account of poverty among white working-class people at the turn of the 20th century in the United States. But Francie Nolan is also a girl who loves books, libraries, and an idealized view of what formal schooling will be. Yet, "before school, there had to be vaccination," the narrator explains. "That was the law":

> When the health authorities tried to explain to the poor and illiterate that vaccination was a giving of the harmless form of smallpox to work up immunity against the deadly form, the parents didn't believe it.... *Some foreign-born parents refused to permit their children to be vaccinated* [emphasis added]. They were not allowed to enter school. Then the law got after them for keeping the children out of school. A free country? they asked. (Smith, 1947, pp. 143–144)

Left alone by their working mother, Francie and her brother, Neeley, must go for their vaccinations, prodded only by a neighbor who rouses them from playing in the dirt and mud. Francie suffers through not only the shot itself, but also the doctor's insensitive and classist criticism: "Filth, filth, filth, from morning to night. I know they're poor but they could wash. Water is free and soap is cheap. Just look at that arm nurse" (Smith, 1947, p. 146). Despite the trauma of the vaccinations and the class-shaming by the doctor, "Francie expected great things from school" (Smith, 1947, p. 151). However, "Brutalizing is the only adjective for the public schools of that district around 1908 and '09. Child psychology had not been heard of in Williamsburg in those days" (Smith, 1947, p. 153). That "brutalizing" included:

The cruelest teachers were those who had come from homes similar to those of the poor children. It seemed that in their bitterness towards those unfortunate little ones, they were somehow exorcizing their own fearful backgrounds. (Smith, 1947, p. 153)

A century plus a decade since this novel, and I must acknowledge there is a disturbing series of patterns that remain, including the anti-vaccination movement as well as a significant portion of parents who find public schools unresponsive to the needs of specific populations of students. History, then, is repeating itself.

When I was reading Smith's novel, I was drawn to some comparisons when I first encountered the mainstream media's uninformed fascination with the science of reading: "What Parents of Dyslexic Children Are Teaching Schools About Literacy" from PBS News Hour (Stark, 2019b). I wondered when I read that headline if mainstream media would ever run this story: What anti-vaccination parents are teaching doctors about disease.

As well, while the current (but still misguided) pro-phonics assault on reading has been spreading for a few years now, *Education Week* has joined the bandwagon driven by parents advocating for their children with dyslexia: "Battle Over Reading: Parents of Children With Dyslexia Wage Curriculum War" (Stark, 2019a) and "College of Education Now Prepares Teachers in the Science of Reading" (Education Week, 2019).

In one article, for example, Stark (2019a) recycles both misinformation about dyslexia—"dyslexia affects 1 in 5 individuals" (para. 3)—and resorts to citing the National Reading Panel (NRP) as a credible report on reading, although at best the report is a politically skewed and incomplete work). In fact, 1 in 10 children are diagnosed, according to Dyslexia International (2014), but many sources suggest the exact percentage ranges from 5% to 17% (National Center for Learning Disabilities, 2017). And contrary to claims about NRP findings, systematic-intensive phonics for all students has also been discredited (Davis, 2013). Yet as Michael Hand acknowledges, "The zeal with which synthetic phonics is championed by its advocates has been remarkably effective in pushing it to the top of the educational agenda; but we should not mistake zeal for warrant" (Davis, 2013, p. 4).

As I have examined and unpacked concerning school choice (Thomas, 2010), we must resist idealizing parental choice, even in regard to those parents' children. The anti-vaccination movement occurring now is grounded in both those parents wanting what is best (in their view) for their children's health and a garbled misunderstanding of vaccinations driven by one deeply flawed study that makes those parents believe they have science on their side:

Lacking the scientific background, in an attempt to protect their children, parents contemplating the risk of vaccine are vulnerable to omission biases by which they are more likely to take the risk of inaction than the risk of action . . .

The anti-vaccine movement appears to be part of a larger trend of discontent and distrust in the established preeminence of scientific evidence over impressions and opinions. A corollary to the discontent is the democratization of health-related decision making, by which stakeholders have an increasingly stronger voice over experts, as well as the dethroning of the Expert. While democratization of health care decision making is cheered by liberals and conservatives alike, its benefits are still to be proven. Decisions in the area of disease prevention require knowledge of the medical field involved and an understanding of statistics, in the absence of which no amount of communication skills and efforts would do any good. (Davidson, 2017, p. 406)

This, I think, is a powerful harbinger of how the current reading war is being perpetuated by rhetoric ("the science of reading") and zeal among parents who seek to democratize the teaching of reading, and as a result, the expertise of literacy educators is erased and replaced by parent will and political caveat. Here are some essential facts being ignored by the avalanche of zeal among some parents of children with dyslexia:

- No student, regardless of special needs such as dyslexia, should be mis-served by our public education system. Parents of children advocating for best practices in the service of their children must be heard, and public schools must respond, attended to, however, by special needs educators and scholars, not the policy demands of the parents or political leaders. "My child must be served" is different than "This is how you will serve my child."
- Reading needs of the general population of students must not be held hostage to the needs of unique subsets of students—especially when the zeal of a few is allowed to overwhelm the expertise of educators and literacy scholars.
- Historically, reading instruction has been a victim of false crisis rhetoric, and current calls for the science of reading is yet another round of systematic-intensive phonics advocacy that cannot serve students well.
- The research base on reading instruction (the actual science of reading including whole language and balanced literacy) *has never rejected phonics instruction*, but each student needs varying degrees of direct phonics instruction, only enough so that the

student begins reading and develops as a reader through holistic experiences such as reading by choice and being read to.

- There has never been a time in the history of formal education in the United States that some have not claimed we have a reading crisis. Never. That crisis rhetoric has usually been driven by those with some ulterior agenda or no expertise in literacy.

- Most of the ways that formal schooling now fails students in terms of reading instruction can be connected to the accountability movement—focusing on ever-changing standards and high-stakes testing as well as imposing prescriptive reading programs onto teachers and students.

Parental zeal in the anti-vaccination movement has spurred measles outbreaks, proving that parental zeal must not be allowed to trump medical expertise. Parental zeal for public schools properly serving students with dyslexia must not be allowed to drive reading policy for all children; this is just as unwarranted even as the consequences may not be so easily exposed.

How to End the Reading War and Serve the Literacy Needs of All Students: An Overview

The chapters that follow are not intended to document how we should or can teach reading. In fact, there is abundant work that has existed since the early 20th century to document the many and varied ways we know we should help foster students as readers from the first days of school to the last. As well, this entire book is working well outside being a how-to on teaching reading or a storehouse of research—even as I *am* advocating that test-driven reading policy and instruction are asking way too little of students and their teachers.

Instead, this is an informative work, focusing on the historical and current reading war, that builds to a framework for moving beyond that war, and as the subtitle states, serving the literacy needs of all students.

Chapter 1 ("A Historical Perspective of the Reading War: 1940s and 1990s Editions") offers a historical overview of crisis responses to reading, focusing on the 1940s (WWII literacy rates of soldiers) and a 1990s report spurred by the National Assessment of Education Progress (NAEP). This historical perspective is often missing from media coverage of reading and reading policy debates and decisions made at the federal and state levels.

In Chapter 2 ("The Twenty-First Century Reading War: 'The Science of Reading,' Dyslexia, and Misguided Reading Policy"), I examine the current science of reading phenomenon in mainstream media driven by mainstream media, Emily Hanford and *Education Week* as key examples, but also fueled by dyslexia advocacy, all of which has manifested themselves in education policy such as adopting grade retention based on third-grade test scores and training teachers in the science of reading.

Chapter 3 ("Misreading Reading: The Good, the Bad, and the Ugly") addresses key concepts and topics that are misunderstood but central to the media coverage of the recent reading war, such as the following: The National Reading Panel (NRP), reading programs, balanced literacy (BL), whole language (WL), phonics, scientific research, grade retention, teacher education, and teacher autonomy.

Finally, in Chapter 4 ("How to End the Reading War and Serve the Literacy Needs of All Students: Shifting Our Deficit Gaze, Asking Different Questions about Literacy"), the following reforms needed to end the reading war will be explored:

- Social policy must be implemented to address inequity and the homes, communities, and lives of children; these socioeconomic reforms must be viewed as central to reading policy.
- The mainstream media must abandon Christopher Columbus and both-sides journalism that addresses education/reading.
- Reading policy must abandon ineffective and hurtful commitments that include standards, high-stakes testing, grade retention, and so on.
- Classroom and school practices must abandon reading programs and silver-bullet approaches to literacy, and teaching must be far more individualized and patient.
- Evidence-based teaching of reading must expand the meaning of "scientific" and evidence.

In the Conclusion ("Science of Literacy: A 36-Year Journey and Counting"), I challenge a narrow view of "science," especially in terms of education and literacy.

As you read the following chapters, I want you to keep some big-picture concerns in mind: What do we ultimately mean when we talk about teaching children to read? And what does it mean for a student to be able to read?

I want you to consider this story from a high school ELA class discussion on capital punishment. As the teacher led a discussion on the death penalty, a student interjected that Texas currently uses decapitation for the death penalty. The teacher paused, and then suggested that this wasn't true. The student hurriedly explained it was true, and that he had proof.

The student took out his smartphone, pulling up an article to show the teacher. The article was from *The Onion*.

Patiently, the teacher informed the student that *The Onion* is satire, to which the student replied, "No, it isn't." Keep in mind that this high school student can pronounce the words in the article; he had read the entire piece.

Are our reading standards, sacred high-stakes tests, and reading programs fostering the sort of students who are critical readers, capable of navigating a complex world better than the student above? Is this reading war in any way addressing that problem?

References

Davidson, M. (2017). Vaccination as a cause of autism—myths and controversies. *Dialogues in Clinical Neuroscience, 19*(4), 403–407. Retrieved from https://www.ncbi.nlm.nih.gov/pmc/articles/PMC5789217/

Davis, A. (2013). To read or not to read: Decoding Synthetic Phonics. *IMPACT: Philosophical Perspectives on Education Policy, 2013*(20), 1–38. https://doi.org/10.1111/2048-416X.2013.12000.x

Dyslexia International. (2014). *Dyslexia international: Better training, better teaching*. Retrieved from https://www.dyslexia-international.org/wp-content/uploads/2016/04/DI-Duke-Report-final-4-29-14.pdf

Education Week. (2019). *College of education now prepares teachers in the science of reading* [video]. Retrieved from https://video.edweek.org/detail/videos/carousel-videos/video/6031615922001/college-of-education-now-prepares-teachers-in-the-science-of-reading

LaBrant, L. (1949). *A genetic approach to language.* Unpublished manuscript, Institute of General Semantics, Lakeville, CT.

National Center for Learning Disabilities. (2017). *Understanding learning and attention issues.* Retrieved from https://www.ncld.org/news/state-of-learning-disabilities/understanding-learning-and-attention-issues#ch1howcommon

Smith, B. (1947). *A tree grows in Brooklyn.* New York, NY: Harper Perennial.

Stark, L. (2019a, May 1). Battle over reading: Parents of children with dyslexia wage curriculum war. *Education Week.* Retrieved from http://blogs.edweek.org/edweek/curriculum/2019/05/Parents_of_children_with_dyslexia_wage_reading_battle.html

Stark, L. (2019b, April 30). What parents of dyslexic children are teaching schools about literacy. *PBS News Hour.* Retrieved from https://www.pbs.org/newshour/show/what-parents-of-dyslexic-children-are-teaching-schools-about-literacy

Thomas, P. (2001). *Lou LaBrant—A woman's Life, a teacher's life.* Huntington, NY: Nova Science.

Thomas, P. L. (2010). *Parental choice? A critical reconsideration of choice and the debate about choice.* Charlotte, NC: Information Age.

Vonnegut, K. (1976). *Slapstick.* New York, NY: Delta.

Acknowledgments

No book attributed to a single author is ever, in fact, the sole work of that writer. This book is a powerful example of that fact.

This is a critique of a many decades-long public debate about reading and literacy. I began as a reader, and then I became a writer also; therefore, literacy doesn't just mean the world to me—it is my world. So I must acknowledge all my teachers, beginning with my mother, and all my students as well as all my friends and colleagues in literacy. Every book is indebted to lovers of books.

I also must acknowledge my National Council of Teachers of English community, notably the 2019 national convention in Baltimore where participants overcrowded a room where I and others presented on the "science of reading," proving the importance of this work.

As well, my virtual community, the Literacy Research and Policy Change page on Facebook, has been a key place for support from many wonderful literacy experts and advocates.

Finally, I am more indebted than I can repay to Diane Stephens, former professor of language and literacy (University of South Carolina), for offering kindly a close-read of this entire book. Her patience, expertise, and guidance are reflected in each page to follow.

Large sections of this book were drafted in blog form over most of 2019; concurrently, I often spent time with my granddaughter Skylar who,

How to End the Reading War and Serve the Literacy Needs of All Students, pages xxi–xxii
Copyright © 2020 by Information Age Publishing

as a kindergartner, is herself coming to language. Along with my grandson Brees, Skylar and all children sit in my heart and mind each time I fight for the critical importance of literacy for every person—even as I check myself, knowing those good intentions are not enough.

1

A Historical Perspective of the Reading War

1940s and 1990s Editions

English educator Lou LaBrant (Thomas, 2001) taught in public schools, for experimental schools, and at the college level over 65 years while also leaving behind a significant body of literacy scholarship from the 1920s into the late 1980s. Her career was nearly as impressive as her demanding attitude. Writing in 1931, for example, LaBrant announced: "The cause for my wrath is not new or single" (p. 245). Her "wrath" was aimed at the rise of the project method in English courses in the early decades of the 20th century.

LaBrant was a strong proponent of John Dewey's brand of progressive education. Even in the early 20th century, however, Dewey's philosophy and classroom practices were often misinterpreted—often oversimplified as a slogan, "learning by doing." Much of the popular response to the project method can be traced not to Dewey but to William Heard Kilpatrick's "The Project Method," which was quite popular after it appeared in 1918.

How to End the Reading War and Serve the Literacy Needs of All Students, pages 1–17
Copyright © 2020 by Information Age Publishing
1

Kilpatrick, in fact, distorted Dewey's version of projects: "As Kilpatrick redefined it, the project was now not simply a way of reorganizing the teaching of, say, science; it became, contrary to Dewey's position, a substitute for science" (Kliebard, 2004, p. 141).

Students working on projects, LaBrant noticed in the 1920s and 1930s, began to replace time students spent reading and writing *by choice*, the practices LaBrant supported for many decades as her contribution to scientific practices in education. LaBrant's research, among research by others, strongly endorsed the power of student choice in reading and writing development. In the 2010s, project-based learning (PBL) is, once again, popular across the United States. And from my perspective, similar to LaBrant's, I have witnessed teachers and students being put in *impossible* teaching/learning situations all in the service of "doing PBL."

LaBrant's "wrath" resonates with me because I have taught in the field of education for almost 40 years now in a constant state of anger because of one of the most disturbing problems that define education—the disconnect between teaching practices and historical perspective. For example, many people now promoting PBL seem to embrace it as an *innovative* approach to teaching. Too often, having no historical lens and being drawn to "new" or "innovative" sets up any practice in education for failure, becoming no more than a fad.

During the early decades of LaBrant's career, the beginning of the 20th century, there was a relatively balanced tension among several competing educational philosophies and theories that included at least two factions using the term "scientific" in dramatically different ways (Kliebard, 2004). Dewey's progressivism, which LaBrant practiced, argued for a day-to-day classroom-based approach often called *action research* (each teacher is a researcher-in-practice with every different class of students). The goal here recognized that students and learning are unique and relative. To teach, Dewey argued, is to experiment, perpetually. What works for one student today may not work for another on that same day, in that same lesson. And what works in a lesson or unit this year may inform a future lesson or unit, but it certainly must never be reduced to a template for future teaching. Dewey's progressivism strongly rejects the "all students must" approach to instruction.

Dewey's practical *scientific* lost, however, to efficiency educators who sought a different type of scientific—one that identifies a fixed prescription for what *good* (effective and efficient) teaching must look like and what *student achievement* must conform to (standardized tests). This view of scientific for instruction is restricted to experimental and quasi-experimental research that has controls, randomized samples, and generalizations. In other words, this type of research seeks to determine what practices direct-ly *cause* student learning, and thus seeks the templates and prescriptions Dewey vigorously rejected. Efficiency education drives the use of standard-ized testing but also reinforces back-to-basics movements in education that believe all learning has essential skills and that learning is mostly sequential and analytic (part-to-whole).

This narrow view of science, I think, has only one compelling quality, ef-ficiency. Here is the same problem with education's pursuit of *the* program, such as PBL or the perfect (or essential) reading program. Design a pro-gram, prove through experimental research what makes the program work, and then anyone can simply implement the prescription and sequenced program for *all students* regardless of their needs or backgrounds. I want to emphasize that these are the components of why some people are drawn to systematic-intensive phonics. As the National Reading Panel report not-ed, "It is common for many phonics programs to present a fixed sequence of lessons scheduled from the beginning to the end of the school year" (Shriver, 2000, pp. 2–97). Systematic intensive phonics programs are more compelling than whole language (WL) or balanced literacy (BL) as guid-ing philosophy because phonics programs appear to be easy to implement.

LaBrant concluded her unpacking of the project method with a key element of how scientific evidence can best work in education. Science at its best requires that we define problems, generate evidence, and then match the solutions to the problems. The project method, LaBrant (1931) noted, was missing that connection as people complained that students were ei-ther not reading or lacking reading ability in order to complete projects:

> That the making of concrete models will keep interested many pupils who would otherwise find much of the English course dull may be granted. The remedy would seem to be in changing the reading material rather than in turning the literature course into a class in handcraft. (p. 246)

No one view of science is the solution, but a complex understanding of both a historical view of teaching and learning as well as the problems we face today can lead to the best possible pursuit of science and avoid the reading war we currently face, a public debate that remains absent that his-torical perspective in ways similar to the renewed interest in PBL.

Looking Back to See Now More Clearly

"Historians often mention World War II as a time when expectations for schooling and literacy really took off," explains Deborah Brandt (2004), "when what was considered an adequate level of education moved from fourth grade to twelfth grade in a matter of a few years" (p. 485). National concerns in the United States about literacy can be traced even further back to literacy tests for soldiers in WWI (Gordon, Ponticell, & Morgan, 1991), when 25% of recruits were deemed illiterate.

While low literacy rates from WWI prompted a greater focus on literacy in U.S. public schools, WWII data on literacy again suggested far too many people in the United States struggled with basic literacy. As Brandt (2004) notes:

> Even more profoundly, though, World War II changed the rationale for mass literacy. Literacy was irrevocably transformed from a nineteenth-century moral imperative into a twentieth-century production imperative—transformed from an attribute of a "good" individual into an individual "good," a resource or raw material vital to national security and global competition. In the process, literacy was turned into something extractable, something measurable, something rentable, and thereby something worthy of rational investment. (p. 485)

From the early to mid-20th century, a powerful dynamic was created among racial integration, military-based measurement of IQ and literacy, and changing expectations for public education.

Brandt (2004) sees those relationships in contemporary education reform beliefs and claims:

> We can find eerie parallels between the selective service system of the midtwentieth century and the public educational system of the early twenty-first century. There is the atmosphere of high anxiety around literacy, rapidly changing standards, an imposition of those standards onto more and more people, a search (largely futile) for reliable testing, a context of quick technological development, a heightened concern for world dominance, and a linking of literacy with national security, productivity, and total quality control. This is what happens when literacy links up with competition, with the need to win the war. It is this competition that justifies the strip mining of literacy, the ranking of skill, the expendability of human potential, and the production of just-in-time literacy. It is the blueprint for the Knowledge Economy. (p. 499)

Announcements of a literacy crisis during WWII are roots of similar cries of *education crisis* from the early 1980s (recall *A Nation at Risk*) until today. And throughout the 20th and into the 21st centuries, the complexities of the problems are ignored in order to force agendas that have less to do with education than with serving larger social and political goals—often ones benefitting those in power at the expense of the poor and the disadvantaged.

Therefore, to understand the essential template of any era's reading war, we should look carefully at one of the most intense versions of the reading war during WWII.

What Shall We Do About Reading Today?

The November 1942 issue of *The Elementary English Review* (a journal of the National Council of Teachers of English) included a provocative piece: "What Shall We Do About Reading Today?: A Symposium" (Betts et al., 1942). The opening editorial comment frames the need for the symposium question:

> Careful students of the teaching of reading have long known that America's illiteracy rate is still alarmingly high, and that many of our people who are not technically illiterate do not read well enough to meet the exacting demands of our times. Now it is revealed that hundreds of thousands of able-bodied men have been rejected for war service because of illiteracy, and many others are unable to perform war duties efficiently because of reading deficiency. Functional illiteracy has become a real war hazard.
>
> *The response of the schools has been to place a new emphasis upon reading instruction* [emphasis added]. In some quarters established objectives of the school have been subordinated to reading skill, even to formal reading drills. In order that teachers may be assisted in attacking the problem intelligently, we turned to a group of America's leading experts on the teaching of reading with the question, "In the light of recent findings that many service men cannot read well enough, what policies and procedures in the teaching of reading should the schools follow?" The following contributions are their answers to this question. Fairly detailed summaries of current research in remedial reading, and surveys of remedial procedures will appear in succeeding issues of the Review. (p. 225)

This symposium offers answers to the question about reading from leading literacy experts of the time: Emmett A. Betts, E.W. Dolch, Arthur I. Gates, William S. Gray (first International Reading Association president), Ernest Horn, Lou LaBrant (former president of NCTE and focus of my dissertation, an educational biography), Holland Roberts, Dora V. Smith (former NCTE president), Nila Banton Smith, and Paul Witty (key figure in the career and life of LaBrant).

Unlike most overstated cries of "educational crisis," this national focus on reading was driven by World War II—a genuine international crisis. But, according to the assembled experts on literacy, this 1942 version of the reading war established that these debates are mostly misinformed, misguided, and driven by beliefs instead of evidence.

Betts, in the opening piece, notes an important fact about student illiteracy drawn from a report by then First Lady Eleanor Roosevelt: "One of the students had only four months of schooling, another was foreign born, some came from sections of the country where educational opportunities were meager, and so on. In short, the First Lady's report emphasized the *lack of educational opportunity* [emphasis added] rather than the questionable quality of instruction" (Betts, et al., 1942, p. 225). Before detailing reading problems and possible solutions—including recognizing shortages and shifts in teacher availability—Betts makes a powerful claim:

> In a democracy, the people get the kind of schools they want.... In a democracy, the quantity and quality of educational opportunity is a product of what people want, and what they want is to no small degree conditioned by the educational leadership they have elected to follow. (pp. 225–226)

Relevant to contemporary concerns about *uniform* reading instruction for all students and hyper-focusing on third-grade reading, Betts cautions against overreactions in 1942 because of the state of real-world classrooms:

> Less than a decade ago, the typical school administrator prescribed the same textbooks for *all* [emphasis in original] the children of a given grade regardless of capacities, abilities, interests, and needs. The teacher, then, felt obliged to hold school in terms of a rigid time schedule and to provide instruction only by means of single sets of basal textbooks. For example, all children in third grade were required to use third grade readers, third grade spellers, third grade arithmetic books, and to *memorize* [emphasis in original] the same prescribed list of poems. This was regimentation with a vengeance which produced disabilities, frustrations, a lack of interest, and so on.

> The facts within a classroom do not square with typical educational practices of a decade ago. First grade entrants present wide differences in respect to chronological age, mental age, language facility, background of information, etc. At the end of the first year, children vary from those who are not ready for systematic instruction in reading to those who read as well as the average third-grader. At the beginning of the third grade, a few children are still not ready for systematic instruction in reading while others can read as well as the average fifth-grader. At the beginning of the fifth grade, the reading abilities will typically range from "pre-primer" level to a substantial high school level. From these findings, it is clear that *education increases the range of reading abilities and therefore necessitates differentiated instruction* [emphasis in original]. (Betts, et al., 1942, p. 226)

Betts expresses a century-long argument among teachers of writing; students learn to read at varying rates and through different instructional practices (as well as because of experiences outside of their formal schooling).

Another compelling voice included in this question is William S. Gray, who begins his entry by confronting the national debate itself:

> During a period of national crisis, our weaknesses—educational as well as material—as well as our strength, stand out in striking relief. It is no secret that during the past few months, the *efficiency of our educational system* [emphasis added] has been challenged from top to bottom. Facts have been reported, for example, which indicate that millions of our youth who have gone to school are unable to read sufficiently well to be classified as literate. Military authorities condemn high schools and colleges because of the incompetence of trainees in mathematics and physics. Upper grade, high school, and college teachers place blame on the lower schools for failure to teach pupils to read and study effectively. Furthermore, teachers, parents, librarians, and the press deplore the low level of reading interests and tastes exhibited by a vast majority of school children. (Betts, et al., 1942, pp. 234–235)

Gray then confronts the responses to this national outcry about the teaching of reading, one of which resonates with the current reading war couched in the language of "the science of reading":

> A second attitude which is equally objectionable is illustrated in recent editorials which maintain that current deficiencies in reading are the product of "pseudo- scientific bungling" and the innovation of so-called progressive methods of teaching. The solution advocated by one editor was the elimination of "impractical non-essentials," which were not defined, and of "undisciplined dabbling with practical essentials." The implication of these vague criticisms is that recent innovations in teaching reading have been adopted without due consideration of essentials and of methods of achieving desired ends. Such assumptions are as unsound and merit no more consideration than a purely defensive attitude. (Betts, et al., p. 235)

It seems even in the 1940s many people believed there was a settled "science of reading" that the educational establishment was carelessly ignoring.

Along with refuting these typical false charges, Gray builds to a powerful closing argument:

> A common error on the part of those who modify their reading programs is to adopt one or more reforms, such as the provision of much free reading, and neglect other aspects of reading that need specific attention....

> If the discussion thus far has achieved its purpose, it should be clear that current deficiencies in reading are not the product of "pseudo-scientific fumbling" or the use of progressive reforms, as some would have us believe. They are due in large measure either to the continued use of traditional patterns of teaching or to failure to provide a *well-balanced* program

of reading activities that harmonize with progressive trends. (Betts et al., 1942, pp. 236–237, emphasis in original)

Since the 1940s, then, people in the United States have periodically identified a reading crisis, blamed schools and teachers, and focused on drawing a stark line between careless instruction and some sort of scientific proof of how better to teach reading. This narrative has always been *incomplete* and *distracting*, and as I will detail again later in this chapter, the United States simply has never had a decade in the 20th or 21st centuries when this same pattern hasn't been in play. In short, *regardless of how reading has been taught*, no one in the United States has ever been satisfied with reading achievement by students.

Few people then or now challenge the problems with the reading war patterns better than Lou LaBrant, who takes a much more direct approach than others in the symposium in her response:

Within the past ten years we have made great strides in the teaching of purposeful reading, reading for understanding (the kind of reading, incidentally, which the army and navy want). Nevertheless, we hear many persons saying that the present group of near-illiterates are results of "new methods," "progressive schools," or any deviation from the old mechanical procedures. They say we must return to drill and formal reciting from a text book. (Betts et al., 1942, p. 240)

However, LaBrant then completely discredits that argument:

1. *Not many men in the army now have been taught by these newer methods* [emphasis in original]. Those few come for the most part from private or highly privileged schools, are among those who have completed high school or college, and have no difficulty with reading.

2. While so-called "progressive" schools may have their limitations, and certainly do allow their pupils to progress at varied rates, above the second grade their pupils consistently show superior ability in reading. Indeed, the most eager critics have complained that these children read everything they can find, and consequently do not concentrate on a few facts. *Abundant data now testify to the superior results of purposeful, individualized reading programs* [emphasis in original].

3. The reading skills required by the military leaders are relatively simple, and cause no problem for normal persons who have remained in school until they are fourteen or fifteen. Unfortunately the large group of non-readers are drop-outs, who have not completed elementary school, come from poorly taught and poorly equipped schools, and *actually represent the most conservative and backward teaching in the United States* [emphasis in original]. (Betts et al., pp. 240–241)

Many progressives such as LaBrant both taught in K–12 classrooms and published high-quality statistical research to support their practices; she exaplains, in the second point above, that scientific research actually supported the reading instruction many were falsely blaming for poor literacy among military recruits (later in this chapter, see Krashen [2004] on a similar pattern in the 1980s and 1990s).

The reality of literacy in the United States, as well as how reading was or wasn't taught, is *far more complex* than the national debate allowed, LaBrant explained. In her conclusion, LaBrant is passionate and unyielding:

> An easy way to evade the question of improved living and better schools for our underprivileged is to say the whole trouble is lack of drill. Lack of drill! Let's be honest. *Lack of good food; lack of well-lighted homes with books and papers; lack of attractive, well equipped schools, where reading is interesting and meaningful; lack of economic security permitting the use of free schools—lack of a good chance, the kind of chance these unlettered boys are now fighting to give to others* [emphasis added]. Surround children with books, give them healthful surroundings and an opportunity to read freely. They will be able to read military directions—and much more. (Betts et al., p. 241)

In the 1940s, as is true still today, almost all children who live in relative affluence with more than adequate food and healthcare become more than proficient readers even before they enter school, but then also excel in school as well across almost all academic areas. LaBrant targets the exact "lack" that people in the United States refuse to acknowledge in favor of blaming schools and teachers—and teaching methods.

Within five years, LaBrant (1947) penned what would become a refrain of her 6-plus decades as an educator: "A brief consideration will indicate reasons for the considerable gap between the research currently available and the utilization of that research in school programs and methods" (p. 87). In other words, LaBrant embodied a call for a progressive version of scientific evidence to drive classroom instruction, but she was never suggesting the sorts of casual or careless approaches that people use to misrepresent WL or BL, simply because they fall within a progressive tradition.

Finally, worth noting is Nila Banton Smith's contribution, a response that addresses phonics instruction directly, but even in 1942, the phonics debate here looks little different than how it is recycled in every version of the reading war:

> Several years back phonics was over-emphasized through elaborate methods which made use of isolated, purposeless drill procedures which were unsound when evaluated in terms of modern psychology. Because phonics

was improperly taught, a stigma was attached to the whole subject of pho-nics and it was dropped from the curriculum in large numbers of schools throughout the country. The present army recruits were passing through the schools during this period, and probably many of them never acquired methods of attacking new words independently.

Several investigations have recently been conducted which reveal evidence that supports us in the contention that phonics is a valuable aid in develop-ing word recognition ability. It should of course be taught in functional con-textual situations according to pupil needs. And it should be supplemented by practice in using several other methods of attack which are useful in solving new words. (Betts et al., 1942, p. 250)

The phonics debate seems always to center on whether or not phonics is be-ing taught in schools and misunderstanding the important but not singular value of a wide variety of phonics instruction depending on student need. Smith also cites four research studies on phonics from the 1920s, 1930s, and 1940s that phonics instruction must be in the context of a wide array of literacy instruction. But her claim about phonics being dropped through-out the country lacks evidence to verify it—again similar to unsupported arguments in the current reading war.

The 1942 version of the reading war addressed viewing reading as a set of discrete skills (an earlier version of the simple view of reading) versus hold-ing a very complex view of reading that included recognizing the larger goal of critical literacy. Dora V. Smith, for example, argues: "The improvement of reading at any level of instruction depends upon lifting it out of the realm of mere exercise-doing and placing it on the firm basis' of problematical think-ing and the acquisition of experience and ideas through books" (Betts et al., 1942, p. 244). Overall, the question about reading raised in the 1940s suffered from the same failures to recognize the problem in order to shape effective and credible solutions that we are confronting in 2020 and beyond.

Reading scholars in the 1940s recognized that many factors determined how well students and adults could read, or how well students and adults were *likely* to read. Many of those factors have always been far beyond the scope of schools to address. But those scholars also knew that students pre-sented a wide range of needs so instructional practices for reading should never be too narrow, too rote, or too disconnected from real-world con-texts. Yet, their pleas fell mostly on deaf ears then.

In fact, the fumbling in the 1940s and today of the reading war is an im-portant snapshot to recognize a tired truism: "Those who cannot remem-ber the past are condemned to repeat it" (George Santayana), and "repeat" it does in the 1990s.

Back to the Future of Reading Instruction: 1990s Edition

The year was 1997 and the topic, of course, was improving a failing education system in the United States. One report from The National Commission on Teaching and America's Future by Linda Darling-Hammond (1997) explains in the Preface:

> This follow-up report, Doing What Matters Most: Investing in Quality Teaching, seeks to gauge the nation's progress toward the goal of high-quality teaching in every classroom in every community. It draws on data about the conditions of teaching that have become available since the original Commission report was released, and it examines policy changes that have occurred. (p. v)

This report has five recommendations that may sound familiar:

  I. Standards for teachers linked to standards for students...
 II. Reinvent teacher preparation and professional development...
III. Overhaul teacher recruitment and put qualified teachers in every classroom...
 IV. Encourage and reward knowledge and skill...
  V. Create schools that are organized for student and teacher success. (Darling-Hammond, pp. 3–5)

Once again, the commission argued that the United States needed better standards for teachers and students, better teacher education, better recruitment of teachers focusing on high quality, better reward systems for teacher expertise and outcomes, and better teaching and learning conditions. Yet, the report also offered some sobering evidence from previous efforts at educational reform:

> Over the last decade, reforms have sought to increase the amount of academic coursework and the numbers of tests students take, in hopes of improving achievement. These initiatives have made a great difference in coursetaking: In 1983, only 14% of high school students took the number of academic courses recommended in A Nation at Risk—4 units in English and 3 each in mathematics, science, and social studies. By 1994, more than half (51%) had taken this set of recommended courses.

> Despite these changes, achievement scores have improved little, and have actually declined slightly for high school students in reading and writing since 1988 (see Figure 3). (Darling-Hammond, 1997, p. 7)

In the context of the reading war, then, look at Figure 1.1 for some important data about reading achievement from 1980 into the mid-1990s. Do you

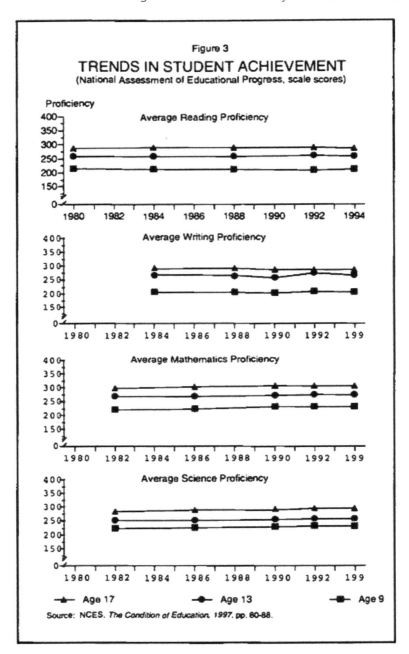

Figure 1.1 Trends in student achievement (National Assessment of Educational Progress, scale scores). *Source:* Figure 3 from Darling-Hammond, 1997, p. 8.

notice anything familiar when we compare the trends shown in Figure 1.1 with fourth and eighth grade reading trends since 1992 (see Figure 1.2)? Reading achievement in the 1980s and 1990s are relatively flat as they have been from 1992 until the present.

While the 1997 report concedes what research has long shown—the largest influences on measurable student outcomes are out-of-school factors (parent income, level of education, etc.)—the focus remains on teacher practices, offering a rare set of correlations between reading scores and reading instructional practices (see the Table 1.1).

Trend in fourth-grade NAEP reading average scores

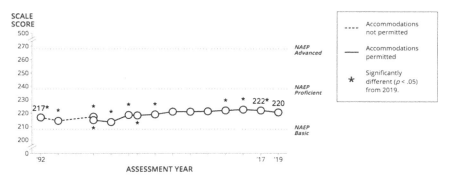

Trend in eighth-grade NAEP reading average scores

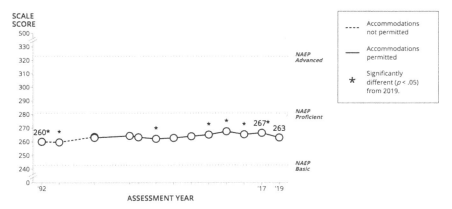

Figure 1.2 Trends in 4th and 8th grade reading since 1992. *Source:* National Assessment of Educational Progress [NAEP] charts. Retrieved from https://www.nationsreportcard.gov/reading/nation/scores/?grade=4 and https://www.nationsreportcard.gov/reading/nation/scores/?grade=8

TABLE 1.1 Correlates of Reading Achievement (Average Student Proficiency Scores, National Assessment of Education Progress, 1992)

Correlates of Reading Achievement	Lower Scores	Higher Scores
Teacher Qualifications		
Level of certification	Substandard or none 214	Highest level 219
Levels of education	Bachelor's degree 215	Master's degree 220
Coursework in literature-based instruction	No coursework 214	Yes coursework 218
Coursework in whole language approaches	No coursework 214	Yes coursework 218
Teaching Practices		
Types of materials used	Primarily basal readers 214	Primarily trade books 224
Instructional approaches	Structured subskills 200	Integrative language 220
Emphasis on integrative reading and writing	Little/no emphasis 211	Heavy emphasis 220
Emphasis on literature-based reading	Little/no emphasis 208	Heavy emphasis 220
Frequency of use of reading workbooks and worksheets	Almost every day 214	Less than weekly 222
Frequency with which students write about what they have read	Less thank weekly 214	Almost every day 221
Frequency with which teachers use reading kits to teach reading	At least once a week 211	Never or rarely 219
Frequency with which teachers take class to library	Never or rarely 209	At least once a week 219
Use of multiple choice tests to assess students in reading	At least once a week 209	Less than monthly 222
Using of short-answer tests to assess students in reading	At least once a week 214	Less than monthly 222
Using of written assignments to assess students in reading	Less than monthly 210	At least once a week 220
Source: 1992 NAEP Trial State Assessment. Darling-Hammond, 1997, p. 12		

Here is where I want to emphasize that, unlike this 1997 report, currently no one has conducted even a correlational graph such as the one above—and no one has conducted scientific research to identify causal relationships—to draw conclusions about 2017 and 2019 NAEP reading scores and instructional practices. Table 1.1 raises some key questions about the current "science of reading" claims about teacher education and the need for systematic intensive phonics (and not WL or BL). Note above that whole literacy practices and training *correlate with higher scores.*

Twenty-plus years after this report from Darling-Hammond have seen at least two significant additional rounds of educational reform, one driven by No Child Left Behind and another sputtering reform movement driven by Common Core State Standards. Just as educational leaders faced in the 1990s, we are today left with the same data problems, notably flat or dismal reading scores, and can only reach for the same recommendations that have never worked before. The five recommendations from 1997 are echoed today by political leaders and the "science of reading" advocates, all blaming teacher education, teacher expertise, and focusing on standards, tests, and programs. And little to nothing is done about food and work security, healthcare, or class size—even though *these conditions combined would dwarf any measurable impact of teacher quality or program/standards quality.*

But also worth noting, in terms of having a historical lens for the reading war, whenever it recurs is that while the Darling-Hammond (1997) report offered positive results connected to WL, critics often point to a major failure of WL from the late 1980s into the 1990s (see more on WL in Chapter 3). This mythology about WL persists until today despite it being discredited by Krashen (2002):

> The Plummet Legend has had serious consequences. It has led to the discrediting of the whole-language approach to literacy and has nurtured a strong movement promoting a "skill-building" approach. I will try to show here both that the evidence does not support this legend and that the legend is inconsistent with the results of studies of literacy development. (p. 748)

The *plummet legend*, however, was used nationwide, and is referenced today, to claim falsely that WL fails students because it bans the teaching of phonics. Yet, as Krashen (2002) shows through more complex research and his own experience with literacy in California:

> So the Great Plummet of 1987–92 never happened. California's reading scores were low well before the California Language Arts Framework Committee met in 1987. Moreover, there is compelling evidence that the low scores are related to California's impoverished print environment. There is also strong and consistent evidence that the availability of reading material is related to how much children read and that how much children read is related to how well they read. A close look at the evidence suggests that the skills-and-testing hysteria that has gripped California and other states has been unnecessary. (p. 752)

What is also important about this version of the reading war is that it also includes false claims around NAEP data, misinformation about phonics instruction and WL, and a failure to acknowledge that reading data are often influenced by a many factors including significant factors outside the walls of schools.

Once the Great Plummet of WL in California during the 1980s and 1990s is unpacked, we must recognize that no one knows if and how WL was actually implemented in classrooms (educational policy does not always mean policies are implemented or implemented well), that the state suffered greatly reduced educational funding, and that the state also experienced high influxes of English language learners. Dozens of factors impacted reading scores in California; therefore using that era to discredit a single factor, WL, is nothing more than seeking an easy scapegoat in order to address a complex problem.

Ultimately today, the "science of reading" and NAEP-crisis rhetoric are doomed because the Christopher Columbus syndrome (thinking you have discovered something that others you ignore or marginalize have known forever) insures that one truism noted above will remain true—those ignorant of history are doomed to repeat it. Today's reading war is just that, back to the future of reading, a 1990s edition recast.

With this historical context in mind, let's consider in Chapter 2 more fully the 2019 version of the reading war driven by a call for "science of reading" and the well-organized and passionate advocates of students with dyslexia.

References

Betts, E., Dolch, E., Gates, A., Gray, W., Horn, E., LaBrant, L., . . . Witty, P. (1942). What shall we do about reading today? A symposium. *The Elementary English Review, 19*(7), 225–256. Retrieved from www.jstor.org/stable/41382636

Brandt, D. (2004). Drafting U.S. literacy. *College English, 66*(5), 485–502. https://doi.org/10.2307/4140731

Darling-Hammond, L. (1997, November). *Doing what matters most: Investing in quality teaching.* Kutstown, PA: The National Commission on Teaching and America's Future.

Gordon, E. E., Ponticell, J. A., & Morgan, R. R. (1991). *Closing the literacy gap in American business: A guide for trainers and human resource specialists.* Westport, CT: Quorum Books.

Kliebard, H. M. (2004). *The struggle for the American curriculum, 1893–1958* (3rd ed.). New York, NY: Routledge.

Krashen, S. (2002). Whole language and the great plummet of 1987–92. *Phi Delta Kappan, 83*(10), 748–753.

LaBrant, L. (1931). Masquerading. *The English Journal, 20*(3), 244–246.

LaBrant, L. (1947). Research in language. *Elementary English, 24*(1), 86–94.

Shriver, E. K. (2000). *Report of the National Reading Panel: Teaching children to read: Reports of the subgroups (00-4754).* Washington, DC: U.S. Government Printing Office.

Thomas, P. (2001). *Lou LaBrant—A woman's life, a teacher's life.* Huntington, NY: Nova Science.

2

The 21st Century Reading War

"The Science of Reading," Dyslexia,
and Misguided Reading Policy

From the end of 2018 and through the first months of 2019, I was like John Proctor in *The Crucible*: "I never knew until tonight that the world is gone daft with this nonsense" (Miller, 1954, p. 66). The nonsense that John Proctor faced was the slow boil that became the Salem witch trials. The nonsense for me? The "science of reading"—sweeping across mainstream media and driving educational legislation in several states in the United States.

My first clue, what I designate as "ground zero" in the current reading war, was a news article, "Hard Words: Why Aren't kids Being Taught to Read?" (Hanford, 2018). But it was several months later before I recognized another key element, the parent movement known as Decoding Dyslexia (Allington, 2019), that merged with what has become Emily Hanford's "science of reading" mantra, creating a compelling new version of the reading war.

How to End the Reading War and Serve the Literacy Needs of All Students, pages 19–56
Copyright © 2020 by Information Age Publishing
19

While some of us may pass off the media obsession with the "science of reading"—*Education Week*, for example, has run story after story throughout 2019—as nonsense, Decoding Dyslexia has directly changed reading and special needs legislation in several states (Allington, 2019). Throughout the late 2010s, there has also been a flurry of third-grade reading legislation often grounded in grade retention requirements (National Conference of State Legislatures, 2019), despite a significant body of research showing that grade retention is, at best, only effective in raising test scores in the short term while overwhelmingly harmful for students in the long term (Jasper, Carter, Triscari, & Valesky, 2017; National Council of Teachers of English, 2015).

Since 2018, then, I have been engaging with this newest reading war, little different from all the versions before (see Chapter 1), even as it adopts new language to mask old arguments.

Misreading the Reading War Again (and Again)

The branding slogan of the current reading war is the "science of reading," and the media messiah for this movement is Hanford (2018), whose initial article reveals in its framing blurb the central arguments dominating this round of yet another invented reading crisis:

> Scientific research has shown how children learn to read and how they should be taught. But many educators don't know the science and, in some cases, actively resist it. As a result, millions of kids are being set up to fail.

First, as I detail in Chapter 1, the claim that educators are not teaching reading as they should is well into its eighth decade of crisis rhetoric. For another historical example, Hanford's discovery and arguments are essentially the same as the classic example from the mid-20th century: Rudolf Flesch's *Why Johnny Can't Read* published in 1955. Saying children in the United States can't read has always sold on the popular market.

Hanford's award-winning journalism on reading established a slogan that has gained momentum in the media as states increasingly point to poor reading scores and adopt new reading legislation. Despite the "science of reading" being settled, Hanford claims, teachers do not know or use that science because teacher education has failed to teach it. Absent in this reading war is the same omission LaBrant confronted in the 1940s; there is little mention of poverty, access to books, or student/teacher ratios, for example. Reading achievement in this reading crisis is primarily attributed to teacher expertise (or claims of teachers lacking that expertise) and inadequate teacher practice—an argument that was dominant during the Obama administration, but has *decades of scientific research* showing that teacher quality and practices accounts for only about 10–15% of student achievement (Di Carlo, 2010). Also absent in these arguments focusing on reading achievement and teacher impact is a similar research base showing that test scores are overwhelmingly a reflection of socioeconomic factors in students' home, communities, and schools (Thomas, 2012).

Hanford's misrepresentations and incomplete picture of reading research are being repeated throughout mainstream education journalism that has embraced the "science of reading," from NPR and PBS to *The New York Times*. This explosion of interest in the "science of reading" has failed to acknowledge that Hanford and other education journalists cite *uncritically* flawed and even debunked sources—the National Reading Panel (NRP), flawed (Garan, 2001), and reports from the National Council on Teacher Quality (NCTQ), debunked, interestingly, because their research methods do not meet the standards of scientific research.

The conclusions from the NRP (National Reading Panel, 2000a; National Reading Panel, 2000b) were at best an incomplete overview of the "science of reading," but those conclusions also were not a blanket endorsement of systematic-intensive phonics, one of the main elements emphasized about the "science of reading." Hanford's misreading of the NRP, in fact, fulfills a warning from a *member of the panel*, Joanne Yatvin (2003), who cautioned:

> Although I still maintain, as I did in my minority view, that the NRP report is not complete or objective enough to stand as the foundation for reading instruction in America's schools, I believe that its findings, reported accurately, do provide some valuable guidance for schools and teachers. (para. 5)

Yatvin clarified almost two decades ago in the same publication promoting Hanford's misinformation, *Education Week*, that the NRP did not fully investigate (and thus did not discredit) whole language (WL) since much of the qualitative studies on WL were omitted from the NRP investigation and offered only a restricted support for systematic-intensive phonics in Grade 1 (see Chapter 3 for a fuller examination of the NRP).

Hanford and other journalists also reference NCTQ, a partisan think tank exclusively committed to discrediting teacher education. NCTQ's reports, when reviewed (Thomas & Goering, 2016), are shown to be deeply flawed in methodology and typically misread or misrepresent research in order to reach their intended conclusion—teacher education is a failure (as reading instruction, apparently, has always been). NCTQ lacks scholarly credibility, but the organization has learned how to manipulate the current state of press-release journalism that simply reports uncritically on whatever aggressive organizations are willing to feed journalists desperate for online traffic.

NCTQ benefits from a disproportionate voice in education reform because they aggressively promote their reports through press releases. But NCTQ's aggressive advocacy also benefits from the current standards of education journalism that focuses on reporting while refusing to investigate the credibility of what is being promoted. *In other words, mainstream journalism is eager to report what NCTQ is claiming, but refuses to assist the readers in understanding whether or not those reports are, in fact, credible.* Mainstream media have a long history of preferring less credible reports on education over high-quality scholarship, in fact (Malin & Lubienski, 2015; Molnar, 2001; Yettick, 2009).

Along with relying on discredited and flawed sources, Hanford's article misrepresents WL and balanced literacy (BL). A more accurate understanding of WL and BL (see Chapter 3) exposes why some are eager to misrepresent both (falsely claiming they do not allow phonics instruction) and endorse systematic-intensive phonics-first *programs*: WL/BL are philosophical guidelines for literacy and teaching literacy (not programs), but phonics-first *programs* are veritable cash cows for textbook companies and the testing industry. To understand that connection, we need look only to fairly recent history to be reminded that the NRP and No Child Left Behind combined for the Reading First textbook scandal under the George W. Bush administration. States recognized that funding was directly linked to adopting specific basal reading programs from preferred publishers (The Reading First Program's Grant Application Process, 2006; Trelease, 2006). In other words, one element of the reading war in the United States that tends to be under-investigated is the commercial interests in keeping the reading crisis alive so more programs, textbooks, and tests can be sold.

To emphasize briefly here, *WL and BL are research-based philosophies of literacy and reading that include the teaching of phonics as well as a broad body of research.* And thus, essentially *no one in literacy recommends banning direct phonics instruction.* WL and BL, however, do stress the need for the right amount and right time for direct phonics instruction (depending on student needs) and recognize that all students need rich and authentic whole reading experiences to grow as readers (not phonics rules, not phonics worksheets, not phonics tests, and certainly not time spent pronouncing nonsense words). Broadly, WL and BL raise cautions about overemphasizing decoding and phonemic awareness to the exclusion of comprehension and critical literacy.

Next, however, is the real paradox to any previous and the current reading war.

Formal schooling has likely never taught reading well to all students, especially to the most vulnerable students. Historically, middle-class and affluent students have likely come to school already capable of reading because of ample access with books; yet, impoverished children, children acquiring English as a second language, and special needs students have always been *identified* as less developed as readers once entering school and have been provided more often with direct instruction in reading provided by schools. Little of that has much to do with teacher education or teacher buy-in because these are social issues that exist beyond the walls of U.S. schools. Again (see Chapter 1), LaBrant often confronted the gap between good research and practice expressed throughout a career in literacy from the 1920s into the 1970s. Of course, the key point is *why* are we as a society failing our students and everything we know about teaching reading? And why do journalists and political leaders misunderstand over and over these failures?

Part of the problem with the focus on the relationship among teacher quality, reading research, and the influence of socioeconomic factors in students' lives and schooling is that this is a very complex relationship. Stated directly, teacher quality certainly matters in that all students deserve certified and experienced teachers; more experienced and better educated teachers can be correlated with higher student achievement. However, in the United States middle-class and affluent students are the ones more likely to have certified and experienced teachers while also benefiting from advanced courses with low student–teacher ratios. And the final complicated fact is that teacher quality is unlikely to result in measurable student achievement as long as those socioeconomic factors are not addressed. The result of these relationships in the United States is that students in poverty, ELL students, and students with special needs experienced multiple disadvantages of negative out-of-school factors; underfunded schools and un-/under-certified, inexperienced teachers; and skill-and-drill instruction that seeks to raise test scores (Gennetian et al., 2012).

A short but important point, then, is that of course teacher quality matters, and an urgent reform needed in U.S. education is to address both student access to high-quality teachers (certified and with experience) across socioeconomic status of those students and teaching/learning conditions (such as student–teacher ratios) and access to high-quality courses and programs for all students.

One powerful reason for not teaching reading well over the last 4 decades is the accountability movement grounded in standards and high-stakes tests. Reading instruction (like writing instruction) has been driven by a Gerald Bracey (2006) truism: What is tested is what is taught. Because of accountability, reading has become by default the skills associated with reading that are efficiently tested, and in that context, phonics as discrete skills is both easily tested and taught to meet how reading is tested. For example, much of the advocacy for systematic-intensive phonics over the past couple decades has been grounded in students being able to pronounce nonsense words (words such as "jat" that do not exist in English) by applying phonics rules. Many in literacy doubt that focusing on nonsense words and pronunciation are effective ways to encourage and develop students as strong readers, however.

Test reading is measurable, but it is a pale reflection of deep and authentic reading, and no measure at all of any student's eagerness to read. Because of the accountability movement, then, and because of high-pressure textbook reading programs designed to address accountability, we have for decades ignored a significant fact of research on reading: the strongest indicator of reading growth in students is access to books and time to read by choice, not phonics programs (Krashen, 2013).

But K–12 teachers are not the only scapegoats in the "science of reading" reading war today. So are the educators in teacher education. Full disclosure: I have been working in teacher education for nearly two decades, after 18 years teaching high school English in public school. But, I am also the first to admit teacher education fails teachers and education in many of the same ways that we have historically failed students in reading; teacher education is also governed by standards and accountability that detract from important instruction and experiences for those learning to teach. The certification process and the accreditation process are fatal distractions from the potential power of a degree in education, one authentically grounded in a rich and diverse body of philosophy, theory, and research.

Teacher education, however, is not the central problem either because whether or not we are teaching reading research and practices correctly is *irrelevant*; teacher candidates overwhelmingly report that once they are in the classroom, they are told what to do and how—what they know from teacher education is secondary to the mandated reading program of their schools and the need to address and raise test scores regardless of the quality of those tests.

Despite its significant influence, Hanford's article is not a powerful call, then, for teaching students to read. It is a standard example of recycling the patterns of the reading war while being unaware that all of this has happened several times in the past already. Ironically, a bit of time on an Internet browser and *reading* could have produced a much different "ground zero" report on reading in the United States.

The Big Lie About the "Science of Reading"

Social media can also be a powerful window into how we think about and discuss education. The current reading war has been fueled significantly by social media, in fact, empowering parents and advocates for students with dyslexia armed with a compelling refrain, the "science of reading." In many ways, the reading war fits perfectly into Twitter and Facebook, even though it has its roots many, many decades before either were created.

One problem with public debates about education is that political, public, and parent voices often lack experience and expertise in education as well as any sort of historical context, even though they all are deeply passionate about their good intentions. As noted in Chapter 1, those who have studied the history of education, and specifically the many versions of the reading war, know that there has never been a decade in the last 100+ years without political and public belief in a reading crisis. However, one doesn't need a very long memory to recognize that if we currently are (finally?) having a reading crisis, it comes in the wake of almost two decades (nested in a larger 4 decades of accountability birthed under Ronald Reagan) dedicated to *scientifically based education policy*, specifically reading policy driven by the NRP (Thomas, 2013). In the early 2000s, the NRP was promoted as a long-absent clearing house of high-quality evidence on teaching children to read.

Concurrent now with the media fascination with Hanford's the "science of reading" is a move within colleges of education to shift reading away from literacy experts and into the purview of special needs, treating all reading instruction as something like remediation or a learning disability. As I mentioned above, I noticed in early 2019 a very odd relationship on social media: a post on a community Facebook page for advocates of education that was linked to a dyslexia Facebook page promoting Mississippi's increased NAEP scores in reading from 2017.

The Facebook message included with the image shown in Figure 2.1 included dramatic arguments: Mississippi has somehow found the science of reading and is excelling in ways South Carolina (my home state) refuses to do. At that time, I had read and responded to Hanford's "science of reading" article, but I was not aware of Decoding Dyslexia or the groups' influence on reading policies across the United States (Allington, 2019)—although I had worked hard to stop and have repeatedly criticized South Carolina's Read to Succeed, punitive reading legislation that is grounded in third-grade test

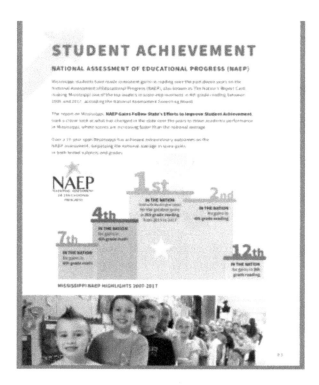

Figure 2.1 Mississippi Department of Education promotional material for 2017 NAEP reading scores.

scores in reading and the threat of grade retention. Because of my background in the relationship among poverty, race, and standardized testing (Thomas, 2012), and NAEP specifically (Schmidt & Thomas, 2009), I was immediately skeptical of these Facebook claims about Mississippi.

Here is the short version of my critique of the claims made about Mississippi by dyslexia advocates: In 2017 NAEP data, Mississippi is slightly ahead of South Carolina in fourth-grade reading (both states remain near the bottom and below the national average), but South Carolina is slightly ahead of Mississippi in eighth-grade reading (again, both near the bottom and below the national average; see Figures 2.2 and 2.3).

While Mississippi was promoting gains (accurately), the data remain clear that high-poverty states tend to score low on standardized testing while more affluent states tend to score higher. What is extremely important to note is that some traditionally low scoring states have adopted methods (test-prep, reading programs focused on raising test scores, and grade

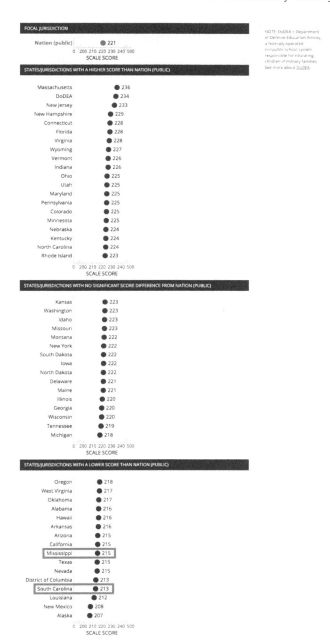

Figure 2.2 Average score comparison between nation (public) and states/jurisdictions in fourth-grade NAEP reading: 2017. *Source*: Chart from NAEP https://www.nationsreportcard.gov/reading_2017/states/scores/?grade=4

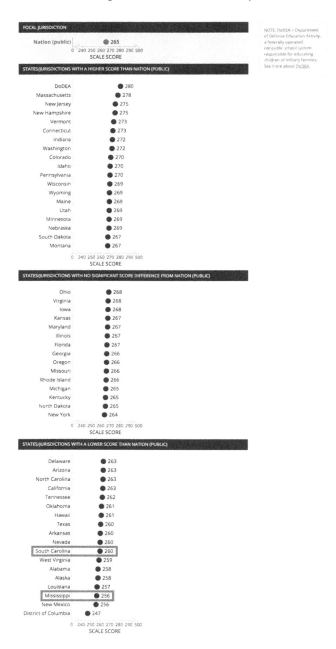

Figure 2.3 Average score comparison between nation (public) and states/jurisdictions in eighth-grade NAEP reading: 2017. *Source*: Chart from NAEP https://www.nationsreportcard.gov/reading_2017/states/scores/?grade=8

retention) that increase test scores *short term* (making for political propaganda), but those gains have proven to be a mirage, disappearing in the span between third/fourth-grade tests to eighth-grade tests and then high school (Jasper, Carter, Triscari, & Valesky, 2017).

So at that point, I became aware of a new reading war that once again raised mostly tired questions: Is there a reading crisis in the United States? And if so, is that crisis somehow the result of refusing to implement the science of reading? First, the questions being raised now must acknowledge that the "science of reading" is code for systematic-intensive phonics and is intended as an antidote to misleading attacks on BL as well as WL. As discussed in Chapter 1, the current reading war is substantially the same as the attack on WL in the 1990s.

This isn't particularly simple or as compelling as a reading crisis or using the term the "science of reading," but let's detail why this recent round of the reading war is misguided and misleading:

- NAEP, promoted as The Nation's Report Card, is a national testing process that chooses random samples of students from the states (not all students) and gathers data periodically (not every year). NAEP data, then, are large bodies of information to draw broad or general conclusions. This sort of standardized testing is not the same as state-based accountability exams that impact all students in that state. NAEP testing tends to have so-called higher standards for success than state testing (all testing sets unique "cut scores" for each level of achievement used in that test reporting), but NAEP data are intended to support comparing states and to provide each state with longitudinal data (over many years) to evaluate progress. It is important that anyone using a set of test data makes sure the data match the sorts of claims anyone is making. For example, there are no mechanisms in place to claim that NAEP data reflect teacher practices or teacher education effectiveness; the test is simply not designed for those evaluations. For comparison, although the media enjoy making these claims, SAT data are not evaluations of any state's educational quality, and SAT data are not accurate statistics for comparing all states.
- Standardized tests of reading are only approximations of reading, typically they reduce reading to a series of separate skills that test designers claim *add up to* reading. This is at least inadequate, if not misleading. Some standardized tests of early reading focus too heavily on decoding and not enough on comprehension. No

standardized test measures eagerness and joy for reading, as well; nearly none address critical literacy.

▪ Raising reading test scores is a teacher's or school's primary or exclusive goal that typically cheats all students. Raising test scores on average is a statistical game that misses the goal of improving reading but also loses the value of any single student in the pursuit of raising an average.

▪ Achieving test score gains when a state is low scoring is much easier than making gains when a state is high achieving. Although this must also come with a caution that standardized test scores remain mostly (about 60% or more) a reflection of socioeconomic status and not achievement.

▪ Adopting, implementing, and staying focused on any reading program—whether they are phonics intensive or claim to be BL or WL—are very common practices, but completely flawed approaches to literacy. Too often, teachers are charged with implementing the program regardless of student needs or outcomes. *Access to books in the home and choice reading remain the strongest predictors of increased reading and reading achievement.*

▪ Ultimately, if we insist on using reading test scores to judge the quality of teaching reading in any state or the country, we must acknowledge that how students are being taught is both almost impossible to identify and completely impossible to characterize as one standard practice. In fact, no one involved in the current "science of reading" reading war has conducted scientific research to identify reading instruction being implemented or how those practices impact NAEP reading scores.

▪ Most important is the fact that standardized test scores of reading reflect a large number of factors, with teaching practices only one (probably small) causal factor.

To that last point, consider Table 2.1 which shows a matrix of 2017 and 2019 NAEP reading scores (4th/8th) along with the poverty rate in each state, the African American population percentage, and the Hispanic/Latinx population percentage as well as reading policy linked to grade retention. These data portray a much more complex picture of the reading problem, and resist the distraction that how students are being taught reading is cheating students, who could be saved simply by the "science of reading."

The "science of reading" version of the reading war, then, is a big lie, but it is also a huge and costly distraction from some real social and educational problems. Relatively affluent states still tend to score above average

TABLE 2.1 Matrix of 2017 and 2019 NAEP Reading Scores

Rank	State Federal District or Territory	Poverty Rate (by household income)	4th Grade NAEP 2017	8th Grade NAEP 2017	4th Grade NAEP 2019	8th Grade NAEP 2019	% African American Population 2010	% Hispanic/ Latinx Population 2016	Grade Retention (REQUIRED) Legislation
1	New Hampshire	9.2%	229^	275^	224^ (< 2017)	268^ (< 2017)	1.1%	3.5%	
2	Maryland	10.4%	225^	267	220 (< 2017)	264^ (< 2017)	29.4%	9.8%	
3	Wyoming	10.6%	227^	269^	227^	265^ (< 2017)	0.8%	9.6%	
4	Connecticut	10.8%	228	273^	224^ (< 2017)	270^ (< 2017)	10.1%	15.7%	√
5	North Dakota	11.1%	222	265	221 (< 2017)	263 (< 2017)	1.2%	3.5%	
6	New Jersey	11.1%	233	275^	227^ (< 2017)	270^ (< 2017)	13.7%	20.0%	[allowed]
7	Minnesota	11.4%	225^	269^	222^ (< 2017)	264 (< 2017)	5.2%	5.2%	[allowed]
8	Alaska	11.4%	207–	258–	204– < 2017	252– (< 2017)	3.3%	6.9%	[allowed]
9	Hawaii	11.5%	216–	261–	218 (> 2017)	258– (< 2017)	1.6%	10.3%	
10	Massachusetts	11.7%	236	278^	231^ (< 2017)	273^ (< 2017)	7.9%	11.4%	
11	Virginia	11.8%	228^	268	224^ (< 2017)	262 (< 2017)	19.4%	9.0%	

(continued)

TABLE 2.1 Matrix of 2017 and 2019 NAEP Reading Scores (Continued)

Rank	State Federal District or Territory	Poverty Rate (by household income)	4th Grade NAEP 2017	8th Grade NAEP 2017	4th Grade NAEP 2019	8th Grade NAEP 2019	% African American Population 2010	% Hispanic/Latinx Population 2016	Grade Retention (REQUIRED) Legislation
12	Utah	11.8%	225^	269^	225^	267^ (<2017)	1.1%	13.8%	
13	Colorado	12.1%	225^	270^	225^	267^ (<2017)	4.0%	21.3%	[allowed]
14	Vermont	12.2%	226^	273^	222^ (<2017)	268^ (<2017)	1.0%	2.0%	
15	Nebraska	12.3%	224^	269^	222^ (<2017)	264 (<2017)	4.5%	10.6%	
16	Iowa	12.3%	222	268	221 (<2017)	262 (<2017)	2.9%	5.7%	√
17	Delaware	13.0%	221	263–	218 (<2017)	260– (<2017)	21.4%	9.2%	√
18	Wisconsin	13.2%	220	269^	220	267^ (<2017)	6.3%	6.7%	
19	Washington	13.2%	223	272^	220 (<2017)	266^ (<2017)	3.6%	12.4%	
20	Kansas	13.5%	223	267	219 (<2017)	263	5.9%	11.6%	
21	Pennsylvania	13.6%	225^	270^	223^ (<2017)	264 (<2017)	10.8%	7.0%	
22	Maine	14.0%	221	269^	221	265^ (<2017)	1.2%	1.6%	[allowed]

(continued)

TABLE 2.1 Matrix of 2017 and 2019 NAEP Reading Scores (Continued)									
Rank	State Federal District or Territory	Poverty Rate (by household income)	4th Grade NAEP 2017	8th Grade NAEP 2017	4th Grade NAEP 2019	8th Grade NAEP 2019	% African American Population 2010	% Hispanic/ Latinx Population 2016	Grade Retention (REQUIRED) Legislation
23	South Dakota	14.1%	222	267^	222^	263 (<2017)	1.3%	3.7%	
24	Illinois	14.3%	220	267	218 (<2017)	265^ (<2017)	14.5%	17.0%	
25	Rhode Island	14.8%	223^	266	220 (<2017)	262 (<2017)	5.7%	14.9%	
26	Idaho	14.8%	223	270^	223^	266^ (<2017)	0.6%	12.3%	
27	Montana	15.2%	222	267^	222	265^ (<2017)	0.4%	3.6%	
28	Indiana	15.2%	226^	272^	222 (<2017)	266^ (<2017)	9.1%	6.8%	√
29	Nevada	15.4%	215–	260–	218 (>2017)	258– (<2017)	8.1%	28.5%	√
30	Missouri	15.5%	223	266	218 (<2017)	263 (<2017)	11.6%	4.0%	√
31	Ohio	15.8%	225^	268	222^ (<2017)	267^ (<2017)	12.2%	3.6%	√
32	New York	15.9%	222	264	220 (<2017)	262 (<2017)	17.5%	19.0%	
33	Michigan	16.2%	218	265	218 (<2017)	263 (<2017)	14.2%	4.9%	√

(continued)

TABLE 2.1 Matrix of 2017 and 2019 NAEP Reading Scores (Continued)									
Rank	State Federal District or Territory	Poverty Rate (by household income)	4th Grade NAEP 2017	8th Grade NAEP 2017	4th Grade NAEP 2019	8th Grade NAEP 2019	% African American Population 2010	% Hispanic/Latinx Population 2016	Grade Retention (REQUIRED) Legislation
34	Oregon	16.4%	218–	266	218	264 (<2017)	1.8%	12.8%	
35	California	16.4%	215–	263–	216– (>2017)	259– (<2017)	6.2%	38.9%	√
36	Oklahoma	16.6%	217–	261–	216– <2017	258– (<2017)	7.4%	10.3%	[allowed]
37	Florida	16.6%	228^	267	225^ (<2017)	263 (<2017)	16%	24.9%	√
38	Texas	17.2%	215–	260–	216– (>2017)	256– (<2017)	11.8%	39.1%	[allowed]
39	North Carolina	17.2%	224^	263–	221 (<2017)	263	21.5%	9.2%	√
40	South Carolina	17.9%	213–	260–	216– (>2017)	259– (<2017)	27.9%	5.5%	√
41	Tennessee	18.2%	219	262–	219	262	16.7%	5.2%	√
42	Arizona	18.2%	215	263–	216– (>2017)	259 (<2017)	4.1%	30.9%	√
43	West Virginia	18.3%	217–	259–	213– (<2017)	256– (<2017)	3.4%	1.5%	[allowed]
44	Georgia	18.4%	220	266	218 (<2017)	262 (<2017)	30.5%	9.3%	√

(continued)

TABLE 2.1 Matrix of 2017 and 2019 NAEP Reading Scores (Continued)									
Rank	State Federal District or Territory	Poverty Rate (by household income)	4th Grade NAEP 2017	8th Grade NAEP 2017	4th Grade NAEP 2019	8th Grade NAEP 2019	% African American Population 2010	% Hispanic/ Latinx Population 2016	Grade Retention (REQUIRED) Legislation
45	District of Columbia	18.4%	213–	247–	214– (>2017)	250– (>2017)	50.7%	11%	√
46	Arkansas	18.7%	216–	260–	215– (<2017)	259– (<2017)	15.4%	7.2%	√
47	Kentucky	19.0%	224^	265	221 (<2017)	263 <2017	7.8%	3.4%	
48	Alabama	19.2%	216–	258–	212– (<2017)	253– <2017	26.2%	4.1%	[pending]
49	Louisiana	19.9%	212–	257–	210– (<2017)	257–	32.0%	4.9%	
50	New Mexico	20.6%	208–	256–	208–	252– (<2017)	2.1%	48.5%	[allowed]
51	Mississippi	21.9%	215–	256–	219	256–	37.0%	2.9%	√

Note: ^ = Above National Average; – = Below National Average.

or average on reading tests; relatively poor states tend to score below average on reading tests. Some states that historically scored low, under the weight of poverty and the consequences of conservative political ideology that refuses to address that poverty, have begun to implement harmful policies to raise test scores in the short-term for political points.

In 2019 and 2020, there is no reading crisis in the way the "science of reading" advocates are claiming. In 2019 and 2020, BL remains the full science of reading, but it likely does not guide the most common ways teachers are teaching reading (see Chapter 3) because schools are almost exclusively trying to raise scores, not foster students who are eager, joyful, and critical readers.

And while my introduction to this round of the reading war was connected to 2017 NAEP scores, the release of 2019 scores has given the "science of reading" even more momentum.

The Big Lie about the "Science of Reading": NAEP 2019 Edition

After the release of the 2017 NAEP reading scores, states such as Mississippi launched a campaign to celebrate the success of their reading legislation. This effort coincided with states adopting reading legislation driven by dyslexia advocates who promote screening all students for dyslexia and systematic-intensive phonics for all students. With the release of 2019 NAEP data, as expected, Hanford and dyslexia advocates overreacted and misrepresented standardized reading test scores, and dyslexia/phonics advocates continue to cherry pick evidence to reinforce their support of the "science of reading." All in all, these responses to NAEP scores are lazy and incredibly harmful.

Broadly, responses by the media and reading advocates have been overly simplistic, and lacking any effort to tease out in a scientific way *mere correlations from actual causal associations* among student demographics, reading policy (Rose, 2012), reading programs, the actual implementation of policy/programs, NAEP testing quality (how valid is NAEP reading tests for critical reading ability, e.g.), and so on. In a Twitter thread (https://threadreaderapp.com/thread/1189609191398367232.html), I offered the following case (revised for this chapter) against rushing to judgment based on 2019 NAEP reading data:

▪ In 2017, Mississippi overstated claims about their NAEP reading scores, hiding the fact that fourth grade bumps disappeared by eighth grade and that NAEP scores remain mostly correlated with poverty (see the section above).

▪ The 2019 NAEP reading scores are likely to be a reboot of that for Mississippi since fourth grade reading is an outlier among states in terms of *gains* but Mississippi remains about average in fourth grade but very low still in eighth grade reading with scores flat since 2017 (see Table 2.1).

▪ Thus, the only fair things to say about new round of NAEP reading scores (most of which I have detailed above) are as follows:

1. There is *always* a claim of a "reading crisis" in the United States.
2. This claim of "reading crisis" is not impacted, however, by how reading is taught.
3. NAEP scores, like all standardized test scores, are mostly (60% +) correlated to out-of-school factors.
4. NAEP scores are only marginally about student achievement/reading, teacher/teaching quality, or reading program effectiveness.
5. NAEP scores are very pale approximations of reading ability.
6. Recent rounds of NAEP reading scores, however, are revealing how really harmful reading policies (grade retention, systematic-intensive phonics for all) can in the short term raise scores while likely deeply harming reading and readers.
7. Fourth-grade reading score bumps are mirages.
8. The equity gap between rich and poor students and states reflected in NAEP reading scores amplifies the reality in the United States that the rich get richer while the poor get poorer. Wealth equals on average high achievement; poverty equals on average low achievement. Student outcomes are a consequence of social negligence not student ability.

Placed in the context of 2017 NAEP reading test scores and a wider recognition that student characteristics (race, socioeconomic status) are historically and currently the greatest causal factors in student standardized test scores, the fairest argument to make in the wake of NAEP 2019 scores is that the wide variety of reading policies and whether or not those policies are implemented uniformly across any state at all or well (elements that we do not have data to support) cannot be identified as success or failure. *We may, however, be able to suggest that focusing on policy, standards, programs, and high-stakes testing simply does not change measurable reading outcomes in positive ways* (Richards, 2019).

Focusing on Table 2.1, we must admit that the relationships among all of the factors *do not paint any clear picture at all* about the effectiveness of programs or policy (again, even if we *assume* those programs and policies are being implemented at all or well). Anyone using 2019 NAEP test scores to claim grade retention works or systematic-intensive phonics works is simply being deeply dishonest because no one has done any of the necessary work to tease out those claims in a scientific way (random sampling, controlling for non-instructional factors, investigating implementation to policies and programs, etc.). In other words, those advocating for the "science of reading" are making no effort to be scientific themselves in the pursuit of proving if their claims are valid, or not.

If we genuinely believe a change in a few points here or there, comparing entirely different populations of students under ever-shifting conditions both in their lives and in their education are in fact not just statistically significant but real-world *significant*, then we have a wealth of evidence available to suggest that all the standards, testing, and policies are actually degrading student reading achievement. Finally, though, I want to stress, the greatest problem exposed by how the media and dyslexia/phonics advocates are responding to NAEP 2019 is that reading is too often a political and ideological football, and students in real classrooms and real lives are being reduced to making claims at their expense.

Again, at no point over the past 100 years have the crisis and failure arguments about reading achievement been any different than throughout 2019 and into 2020—regardless of how students have been taught to read (including peak years of intensive phonics and jumbled claims of implementing WL). Yet, despite the problems I have identified here, the "science of reading" reading war has chosen the state that shows the rest of the nation how to teach reading, Mississippi—once again heralded by Hanford.

Mississippi Miracle or Mirage?: 2019 NAEP Reading Scores Prompt Questions, Not Answers

There is a disturbing contradiction in the anticipated jubilant response to Mississippi's outlier fourth-grade results from the 2019 NAEP reading test. That contradiction can be found in Emily Hanford's (2019) "There Is a Right Way to Teach Reading, and Mississippi Knows It," using Mississippi to recycle her brand, a call for the "science of reading." Hanford continues her argument grounded in a claim that most students in the United States are being taught reading through methods that are *not* supported by scientific research (code for narrow types of quantitative research that can identify causal relationships and thus can be generalized to all students). However, the contradiction lies in Hanford's own concession about the 2019 NAEP reading scores from Mississippi:

> The state's performance in reading was especially notable. Mississippi was the only state in the nation to post significant gains on the fourth-grade reading test. Fourth graders in Mississippi are now on par with the national average, reading as well or better than pupils in California, Texas, Michigan and 18 other states.
>
> What's up in Mississippi? *There's no way to know for sure what causes increases in test scores* [emphasis added], but Mississippi has been doing something notable: making sure all of its teachers understand the science of reading. (paras. 4–5)

To be fair, *there is a way to know*, and that would be conducting *scientific research* that teases out the factors that can be identified as causing the test score changes in the state. In her missionary zeal for the "science of reading," Hanford (2019) contradicts herself by taking most of the article to imply without any scientific evidence, without any research, that Mississippi's gains are by her implication a result of the state embracing the "science of reading": "In 2013, legislators in Mississippi provided funding to start training the state's teachers in the science of reading" (para. 7).

Let me stress here a couple points.

First, scientific research connecting classroom practices to NAEP test scores is rare, but in the 1990s, comparative data were released as I examined in Chapter 1 (Darling-Hammond, 1997). That research showed a possible link between WL practices and higher NAEP scores—something that Hanford and her "science of reading" followers may find surprising since they routinely claim that WL and BL are not scientifically supported. Therefore, immediately after the release of 2019 NAEP scores is simply far too soon to suggest *any relationship* between classroom practices and NAEP scores. *Hanford's implications about Mississippi are premature and irresponsible to make for journalists, politicians, or advocates for education.*

Second, data from Mississippi include more than fourth-grade 2019 reading scores—if we genuinely want to know something of value about teaching children to read. Mississippi's outlier fourth-grade reading scores are *way more complicated* once we frame them against longitudinal NAEP scores reaching back 20 years as well as eighth-grade reading scores. Figures 2.4–2.7 show more data (all accessible from the NAEP website) we should use to ask questions about Mississippi instead of making rash and unscientific claims.

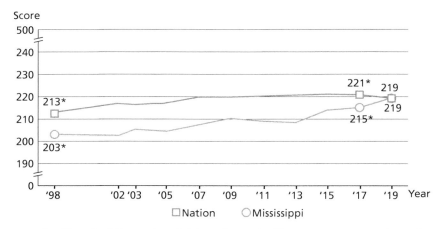

*Significantly different (*p* < .05) from 2019. Significance tests were performed using unrounded numbers.

Figure 2.4 MS NAEP 4th grade reading trends.

Score Gaps for Student Groups

- In 2019, Black students had an average score that was 21 points lower than that for White students. This performance gap was not significantly different from that in 1998 (26 points).
- In 2019, Hispanic students had an average score that was 9 points lower than that for White students. Data are not reported for Hispanic students in 1998, because reporting standards were not met.
- In 2019, female students in Mississippi had an average score that was higher than that for male students by 8 points.
- In 2019, students who were eligible for the National School Lunch Program (NSLP) had an average score that was 24 points lower than that for students who were not eligible. This performance gap was not significantly different from that in 1998 (26 points).

Figure 2.5 MS NAEP 4th grade score gaps.

Here are some questions and a caveat drawn from this larger picture:

▪ If the "science of reading" is the cause of recent gains in fourth-grade reading in Mississippi, how do we explain that Mississippi has seen a trend of increased scores since 1998 and pretty significant increases between 2005 and 2009 (see Box 2.1), well before the policy shift in 2013 identified by Hanford?

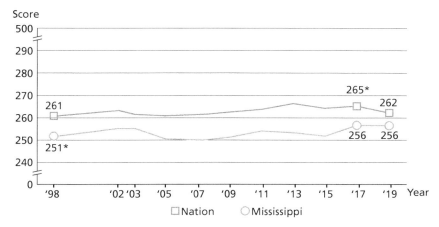

*Significantly different (*p* < .05) from 2019. Significance tests were performed using unrounded numbers.

Figure 2.6   MS NAEP 8th grade reading trends.

Score Gaps for Student Groups

- In 2019, Black students had an average score that was 24 points lower than that for White students. This performance gap was not significantly different from that in 1998 (25 points).
- In 2019, Hispanic students had an average score that was 10 points lower than that for White students. Data are not reported for Hispanic students in 1998, because reporting standards were not met.
- In 2019, female students in Mississippi had an average score that was higher than that for male students by 10 points.
- In 2019, students who were eligible for the National School Lunch Program (NSLP) had an average score that was 25 points lower than that for students who were not eligible. This performance gap was not significantly different from that in 1998 (23 points).

Figure 2.7   MS NAEP 8th grade score gaps.

- ▪ Why does Mississippi still show about the same gaps between Black and White students as well as between socioeconomic classes of students since 1998 if the kind reading instruction practiced is the key factor in changing achievement for *all students*?
- ▪ And a really powerful question concerns eighth grade: Are any fourth-grade gains by Mississippi (or any state) merely mirages since many states with fourth-grade gains see a drop by eighth

grade and since longitudinal eighth-grade scores are mostly stagnant since 1998?

▪ Todd Collins (2019) has raised another important caveat to the fourth-grade reading gains in Mississippi because the state has the highest third-grade retention percentages in the country:

> But Mississippi has taken the concept further than others, with a retention rate higher than any other state [Palmer, 2018]. In 2018–19, according to state department of education reports, 8 percent of all Mississippi K–3 students were held back (up from 6.6 percent the prior year). This implies that over the four grades, as many as 32 percent of all Mississippi students are held back; a more reasonable estimate is closer to 20 to 25 percent, allowing for some to be held back twice. (Mississippi's Department of Education does not report how many students are retained more than once.)

The concern raised about the impact of retention on test scores means that significant numbers of students in states with third-grade retention based on reading achievement and test scores are biologically fifth-graders being held to fourth-grade proficiency levels. Grade retention is not only correlated with many negative outcomes—dropping out, for example (Hughes, West, Kim, & Bauer, 2017)—but also likely associated with "false positives" on testing; as well, most states seeing bumps in fourth-grade test scores also show that those gains disappear by middle and high school (Jasper, Carter, Triscari, & Valesky, 2017).

Ultimately, if anyone wants to argue that how we teach reading in the United States must be grounded only in a narrow view of "scientific" (see Chapter 3 for a discussion of why this is flawed), then any claims we make about the effectiveness of those practices must also be supported by scientific research or at least credible evidence. Despite efforts to make Mississippi a shining example of how all states should address reading policy, we should be using Mississippi (and the 29 states scoring higher) to examine all the factors contributing to why students achieve at the levels they do on NAEP reading tests. Unless, of course, we have real political courage and are willing to admit that NAEP and any form of standardized testing are the wrong ways to make these decisions.

Here's something to think about in that regard: As long as we use standardized testing, we will always have some states above the average, several at the average, and some below the average—resulting in the same crisis rhetoric we see today that is no different than during any decade over the last 100 years. I recommend, instead of all the scientific research needed to make any fair claim, that we stop the testing, make teaching and learning conditions better, make the lives of children and their families in the United States better, and do the complicated daily work it requires to serve the needs of all students (see Chapter 4).

BOX 2.1   NOTE

Hanford (2019) contradicts herself again and opens the door to another question:

> For years, everyone assumed Mississippi was at the bottom in reading because it was the poorest state in the nation. Mississippi is still the poorest state, but fourth graders there now read at the national average. While every other state's fourth graders made no significant progress in reading on this year's test, or lost ground, Mississippi's fourth-grade reading scores are up by 10 points since 2013, when the state began the effort to train its teachers in the science of reading. *Correlation isn't causation* [emphasis added], but Mississippi has made a huge investment in helping teachers learn the science behind reading.

There is an 8-point jump in fourth-grade reading in Mississippi from 2002 to 2009—well before the 2013 policy shift to the "science of reading"—thus how is that explained?

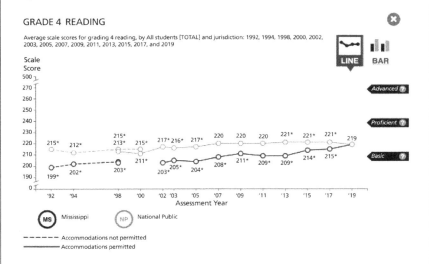

GRADE 4 READING

Average scale scores for grading 4 reading, by All students [TOTAL] and jurisdiction: 1992, 1994, 1998, 2000, 2002, 2003, 2005, 2007, 2009, 2011, 2013, 2015, 2017, and 2019

Also for the record, *causation* is a key component of "scientific," which Hanford espouses for reading, yet she resorts to *correlation* (not scientific) to make her argument.

Another problem with focusing on Mississippi as a model of how to teach reading is that the 2019 NAEP reading scores in fourthgrade are outliers, not only for the state but for the entire nation. Outlier data often do not translate well to generalizations, but seeing Mississippi as a singular model also falls victim to a silver-bullet mentality, one that never serves education well as I examine next.

Resisting the Silver Bullet in Literacy Instruction (and Dyslexia): "There Is No Certifiably Best Method for Teaching Children Who Experience Reading Difficulty"

The Mind, Explained (Netflix), Episode 1, "Memory," introduces viewers to some troubling facts about human memory, transported in the soothing and authoritative voice-over by Emma Stone. This first episode shares a 9/11 memory from a young woman, recalling sitting as a child in her classroom and watching the smoke from the Twin Tower collapse billowing past the window as she worried about her mother working in the city. Her memory is vivid and compelling, but it is also factually wrong—both the detail of the billowing smoke (the window didn't face that direction and the proximity of the school would not have allowed that event to occur) and her mother was not in the city that day. Memory, the episode reveals, is often deeply flawed, as much a *construction* by the person as any sort of accurate recall.

Watching this, I thought about one of the most misinterpreted poems commonly taught in schools, Robert Frost's "The Road Not Taken." This poem, and how people almost universally misread it, is parallel to the problems with memory because people tend *to impose onto text* what they predict or want that text to say; and the verbatim elements of a text, the decoding of words, also depends heavily on *schema*, reader knowledge and experiences as well as the associations that reader has with words and phrases.

(Frost's poem, by the way, is about the significance of choosing, in that when we choose we determine our path. But the poem literally states multiple times that the *paths are the same*; therefore, the poem is not some inspirational poster about making the *unique* choice—although this is the sort of simplistic message many people want to read.)

In the context of dyslexia, advocates calling for systematic-intensive phonics instruction and dyslexia screening for all students as well as the overreaction to the 2019 reading data from NAEP, I believe the memory and poem interpretation phenomena help explain how and why the "science of reading" narrative is so effective while simultaneously being deeply misguided (and misleading). The media and most people find a *single explanation* for reading problems compelling; the argument that more students have dyslexia than are being identified and that one program type (systematic-intensive phonics, usually Orton-Gillingham-based) will cure the low reading achievement crisis matches what people *want* to hear.

The disturbing irony is that those oversimplifying reading challenges and solutions as "the science of reading" are themselves not being very scientific even as they idealize "scientific research." I have argued against this in education for many years and have identified this broadly as *technocratic*, an overreliance on narrow types of measurement in order to control the teaching/learning process in ways that are not possible in real-world classrooms.

The call for reading instruction driven by the "science of reading," then, comes against several problems. First, literacy acquisition and instruction are both inherently messy and chaotic. Despite our seeking efficient and effective methods for teaching reading, mandating that all students develop the same ways and at the same rates is impractical, and even harmful. Concurrent with that unpopular reality, highly structured teaching of literacy is something that is manageable but likely ineffective, and again, harmful.

Narrow expectations for the "scientific" tend to include controlling for external factors and reaching generalizable conclusions—both of which can be inappropriate for guiding the teaching of real students in an actual classroom. Should reading policy and practice be in part *informed* by scientific studies? Of course, but any teacher must frame that research against the needs of each student, needs that may dictate practices outside the parameters of scientific studies. And every teacher has another type of evidence—their practice—to consider.

We must also, recognize, however, that the "science of reading," and the science around dyslexia, are both not as *settled* as some advocates seem to suggest. When we ask the questions being posed now—Is there a reading crisis (distinct from the historical trends of reading test scores)? Is there a dyslexia crisis? Should all students be screened for dyslexia? Should all students receive systematic-intensive phonics instruction?—the answers do not match the current media and advocacy frenzy.

The International Literacy Association's (2016) "Research Advisory: Dyslexia" offers a much different framing of "scientific," in fact:

> Both informal and professional discussions about dyslexia often reflect emotional, conceptual, and economic commitments, and they are often not well informed by research.

First, some children, both boys and girls, have more difficulty than others in learning to read and write regardless of their levels of intelligence or creativity. When beginning literacy instruction is engaging and responsive to children's needs, however, the percentage of school children having continuing difficulty is small (Vellutino et al., 1996; Vellutino, Scanlon, & Lyon, 2000).

Second, *the nature and causes of dyslexia, and even the utility of the concept, are still under investigation* [emphasis added]....

Third, dyslexia, or severe reading difficulties, do not result from visual problems producing letter and word reversals (Vellutino, 1979)....

Errors in reading and spelling made by children classified as dyslexic are not reliably different from those of younger children who are not classified as dyslexic. Rather, evidence suggests that readers with similar levels of competence make similar kinds of errors. This does not suggest a greater incidence of dyslexia, but instead that *some difficulties in learning to work with sounds are normal* [emphasis added]....

[I]nterventions that are appropriately responsive to individual needs have been shown to reduce the number of children with continuing difficulties in reading to *below 2% of the population* [emphasis added] (Vellutino et al., 2000).

As yet, *there is no certifiably best method for teaching children who experience reading difficulty* [emphasis added] (Mathes et al., 2005). *For instance, research does not support the common belief that Orton-Gillingham–based approaches are necessary for students classified as dyslexic* [emphasis added] (Ritchey & Goeke, 2007; Turner, 2008; Vaughn & Linan-Thompson, 2003)....

Some have advocated for an assessment process that determines who should and should not be classified as dyslexic, but this process has been shown to be highly variable across states and districts in the United States, *of questionable validity, and too often resulting in empirically unsupported, one-size fits-all program recommendations* [emphasis added]. (pp. 2–3)

A genuine *science of reading* suggests we should not see a reading crisis in our test scores, and not confuse low test scores in reading with special needs such as dyslexia.

And we must reject calls to adopt singular evaluation processes and reading programs that claim to address the natural development and challenges of 98% of students. All general population students *and* students with special needs deserve rich and diverse literacy instruction that helps teachers recognize their needs in order to foster their natural development over many years (resisting as well the false notion that third grade is a magical moment for all students to attain the same mastery of literacy).

While there are certainly good intentions behind calls for identifying and serving students with dyslexia, the overreaction to reading test scores and oversimplification of "scientific" are pathologizing (mislabeling normal human behavior as a disability to be addressed) and stigmatizing students, and eroding effective teaching and authentic learning. Like memory and poems by Frost, teaching reading and becoming a reader are complicated. Many find that so unpleasant that they have retreated into a mantra that isn't itself very well grounded in evidence, the hallmark of "scientific."

The evidence we use on reading test scores has for at least a century shown us that there really is no normal development of reading at predictable benchmarks and that measurable reading achievement has always been and continues to be a powerful marker for the socioeconomic status of the students tested. Technocrats, however, do not want evidence that is historical and sociological preferring instead to impose a problem and a solution onto the data in ways that are as comforting as a detailed, though false, memory. The current reading war is not only marred by a silver-bullet mentality but also by the zeal of advocates for the "science of reading."

Evidence vs. Advocacy in Teaching Reading: "We Should Not Mistake Zeal for Warrant"

Those of us who are scholars, practitioners, or both in the field of education have suffered a long history of being marginalized as *not really being in an academic discipline* (education as preprofessional, just "teacher training") or *merely classroom teachers*. As someone with experience and expertise as a practitioner (high school English teacher for 18 years) and researcher in education, I often find I still have little authority over issues related to education either with my public work or with my scholarly impact. Imagine if I published a book on psychology, economic, or politics? Think *The New York Times* would scramble to hang on my every word as they did for a psychologist (Daniel Willingham) and a journalist (Emily Hanford) criticizing the teaching reading?

There exists another layer to education that often remains unexamined: K–12 public education is almost exclusively run along partisan political lines through bureaucracy and legislation that is not created by practitioners or educational researchers. Practitioners who teach literacy/reading and literacy/reading scholars are currently under assault again by this new round of the reading war. As has been common in these periodic battles, there really is no war because the so-called "both sides" do not have anywhere near equal power.

As a self-proclaimed reading expert, Hanford, a journalist who directly states she has just recently *discovered* the reading crisis and debate, represents what is essentially wrong with the entire framing of debates about teaching reading as a war—those with the least expertise and most zeal have the most access to promoting their agenda (Malin & Lubienski, 2015). Again, as I included in the "Introduction," Michael Hand warns, "The zeal with which synthetic phonics is championed by its advocates has been remarkably effective in pushing it to the top of the educational agenda; but we should not mistake zeal for warrant" (Davis, 2013, p. 4).

During the current "science of reading" media blitz proclaiming that children *are not* being taught to read because teachers *are not* prepared properly in teacher education and students *are not* receiving systematic-intensive phonics instruction, psychologist (and author of a book on reading) Daniel Willingham (2018) posted on his blog to answer: Just how polarized are we about reading instruction? His post doesn't answer the question very well, but in another moment of karmic irony, Willingham reveals why "we should not mistake zeal for warrant" (Davis, 2013 p. 4). Affecting a tone of being fair and balanced, Willingham (2018) offers six positions on reading:

1. The vast majority of children first learn to read by decoding sound. The extent to which children can learn to read in the absence of systematic phonics instruction varies (probably as a bell curve), depending on their phonemic awareness and other oral language skills when they enter school; the former helps a child to figure out decoding on her own, and the latter to compensate for difficulty in decoding.
2. Some children—an extremely small percentage, but greater than zero—teach themselves to decode with very minimal input from adults. Many more need just a little support.
3. The speed with which most children learn to decode will be slower if they receive haphazard instruction in phonics than it would be with systematic instruction. A substantial percentage will make very little progress without systematic-phonics instruction.
4. Phonics instruction is not a literacy program. The lifeblood of a literacy program is real language, as experienced in read-alouds, children's literature, and opportunities to speak, listen, and to write. Children also need to see teachers and parents take joy in literacy.
5. Although systematic-phonics instruction seems like it might bore children, researchers examining the effect of phonics instruction on reading motivation report no effect.
6. That said, there's certainly the potential for reading instruction to tilt too far in the direction of phonics instruction, a concern Jean Chall warned about in her 1967 report. Classrooms should devote much more time to the activities listed in No. 4 above than to phonics instruction. (paras. 5–10)

He then claims the reading war problem is that competing agendas take either the side of the even or the odd numbered claims—although he adds, "I think all of the six statements above are true."

The problem is a deceptive one because most of Willingham's audience, like Willingham, has no literacy expertise or *practical experience teaching children to read*. For a lay audience, it is unfair to expect anyone to notice that Willingham has misrepresented the so-called factions in the reading war.

One of the leading literacy experts in the United States is Stephen Krashen; in his relentless analysis of research on teaching reading, he notes that the pro-phonics research often is deeply flawed because it presents either garbled or false definitions of WL (or BL) in order to make claims of systematic-intensive phonics being more effective. Willingham's claims about reading instruction and the failures of teaching, teachers, and teacher education can only stand on completely misrepresenting the field of literacy and the so-called debate itself.

Let me frame a different approach to understanding the problem pro-phonics advocates fumble. Here is the real dynamic concerning the teaching of reading in U.S. K–12 education: Teaching reading practices are guided primarily by legislation (with no assurance that legislation is grounded in anything more than *zeal* at the expense of *warrant*) and then driven by the combination of textbook companies appealing to that legislation and accountability structures (most significantly the mandate to raise reading test scores without investigating if those scores are credible representations of reading growth or reading eagerness). That is almost the entire real-world power structure governing how students are taught to read. The power of teachers or teacher educators to know or practice any version of the "science of reading" is dramatically dwarfed by legislation, mandated reading programs, and the dictum, "What is tested is what is taught" (Bracey, 2006).

Well outside the accountability dynamic stand teacher education and literacy/reading researchers, practitioners, and advocates—all of whom, since they have almost no power, are the scapegoats when journalists and psychology professors turn into reading experts and the media provides them disproportionate microphones for their book or in the NYT. I should note, as well, that an even smaller and less powerful group often not acknowledged is literacy experts with a historical perspective, a group that I strongly identify with.

The teaching of reading and the public debate about reading have always been characterized by overblown melodrama and a nearly complete failure to implement what we know about learning to read in K–12 public schools because of partisan political bureaucracy, textbook companies, the massive and growing testing industry, and the misguided influence of non-educators posing as reading and literacy experts. I realize there is nothing sexy about this—there is no war, or crisis—and this message once again will fall on deaf ears because I do not currently hold a position as a journalist, in a psychology department, or as an elected official where I could pander to an uninformed public.

Along with the problems with silver-bullet mentalities and zeal among advocates of the "science of reading" is the practical danger of over-identifying students as having special needs, such as dyslexia, simply because they do not read in a prescribed way and along a prescribed timeline.

On Normal, ADHD, and Dyslexia: Neither Pathologizing, nor Rendering Invisible

In 1973, Elliott Kozuch (2017) explains, "the American Psychiatric Association (APA)—the largest psychiatric organization in the world—made history by issuing a resolution stating that homosexuality was not a mental illness or sickness. This declaration helped shift public opinion, marking a major milestone for LGBTQ equality" (para. 1). Homosexuality in many eras and across many cultures has been rendered either invisible (thus, the "closet" metaphor) or pathologized as an illness (thus, the horror that is conversion therapy [Human Rights Campaign, 2019]).

This troubling history of social responses to homosexuality confronts the inexcusable negative consequences of shame and misdiagnosis/mistreatment against the more humane and dignified recognition that "normal" in human behaviors is a much broader spectrum than either invisibility or pathologizing allows. How we determine "normal" in formal education is profoundly important, and the current rise of dyslexia advocacy as that impacts and drives reading legislation and practice for all students parallels the dangers identified above with rendering invisible or pathologizing children who struggle with reading.

Further, this more recent focus on dyslexia in the context of the "science of reading" reading war looks incredibly similar to the increased diagnosis of ADHD in the United States which was initially left invisible and then pathologized (probably overdiagnosed and heavily medicated). Let's focus first, then, on ADHD, and how the range of responses including *normal, invisible,* and *pathologized* impacts children. In *The New York Times,* Maggie Koerth-Baker (2013) reported:

> The number of diagnoses of Attention Deficit Hyperactivity Disorder has ballooned over the past few decades. Before the early 1990s, fewer than 5

percent of school-age kids were thought to have A.D.H.D. Earlier this year, data from the Centers for Disease Control and Prevention showed that 11 percent of children ages 4 to 17 had at some point received the diagnosis— and that doesn't even include first-time diagnoses in adults. (para. 2)

But here is the problem, Koerth-Baker adds:

> That amounts to millions of extra people receiving regular doses of stimulant drugs to keep neurological symptoms in check. For a lot of us, the diagnosis and subsequent treatments—both behavioral and pharmaceutical—have proved helpful. But still: Where did we all come from? Were that many Americans always pathologically hyperactive and unable to focus, and only now are getting the treatment they need?
>
> Probably not. Of the 6.4 million kids who have been given diagnoses of A.D.H.D., a large percentage are unlikely to have any kind of physiological difference that would make them more distractible than the average non-A.D.H.D. kid. It's also doubtful that biological or environmental changes are making physiological differences more prevalent. Instead, the rapid increase in people with A.D.H.D. probably has more to do with sociological factors—changes in the way we school our children, in the way we interact with doctors and in what we expect from our kids. (paras. 3–4)

For context, when I was exploring the ADHD phenomenon in 2013, I ran across a provocative piece from 2012 about ADHD in France, "Why French Kids Don't Have ADHD," published in *Psychology Today* (Wedge, 2012). Immediately, this spoke to my concern about both pathologizing human behavior that may be within a broader understanding of normal and my skepticism about immediately medicating, instead of addressing diet, environment, and so on.

However, the situation in France is far more complicated as noted in a piece also published by *Psychology Today* in 2015, "French Kids DO Have ADHD," this time acknowledging:

> In other words, it's not that French kids, or Europeans, don't have ADHD, says French child psychiatrist Michel Lecendreux, but that they're *clinically invisible* [emphasis added]. "It's just not very well understood, nor is it very well-diagnosed, nor well-treated." Lecendreux, a researcher at the Robert Debre Hospital in Paris who also heads the scientific commission for the French ADHD support group HyperSupers, told me that his research suggests that fewer than one-third of French children who have ADHD are being diagnosed. (Ellison, 2015, para. 9)

The national language and assumptions around ADHD in France reveal the *power of narratives and cultural responses to human behavior*, any people's perception of "normal." A study by Sébastien Ponnou and François Gonon (2017), in fact, details the pervasiveness of different stories about ADHD in French media:

Abstract: Two models of attention deficit hyperactivity disorder (ADHD) coexist: the biomedical and the psychosocial. We identified in nine French newspapers 159 articles giving facts and opinions about ADHD from 1995 to 2015. We classified them according to the model they mainly supported and on the basis of what argument. Two thirds (104/159) mainly supported the biomedical model. The others either defended the psychodynamic understanding of ADHD or voiced both models. Neurological dysfunctions and genetic risk factors were mentioned in support of the biomedical model in only 26 and eight articles, respectively. These biological arguments were less frequent in the most recent years. There were fewer articles mentioning medication other than asserting that medication must be combined with psychosocial interventions (14 versus 57 articles). Only 11/159 articles claimed that medication protects from school failure. These results were compared to those of our two previous studies. Thus, both French newspapers and the specialized press read by social workers mainly defended either the psychodynamic understanding of ADHD or a nuanced version of the biomedical model. In contrast, most French TV programmes described ADHD as an inherited neurological disease whose consequences on school failure can be counteracted by a very effective medication.

Thus, the interaction among the fields of medicine and psychology, media representations of clinical conditions, and the spectrum along *normal, invisible,* and *pathologized* has profound consequences for children/teens and formal education, notably the teaching of reading.

Currently, mainstream media are building a compelling narrative about the "science of reading" and the needs of children with dyslexia; this is a narrative about children with dyslexia being rendered invisible and the "science of reading" as the medicine necessary to cure that pathology, the illness. However, as the examinations of homosexuality and ADHD above demonstrate, when it comes to the humanity and dignity of children being served by public education, *we cannot tolerate either rendering them and their behaviors invisible or over-pathologizing, and thus, misdiagnosing/mistreating them.*

No child struggling to read should have that struggle rendered invisible, but pathologizing behavior that does not conform to a narrow definition of normal also carries significant negative consequences. A more reasonable approach is simply to *expand the spectrum of normal* while building a supportive environment tempered with patience.

Advocates for universal screening for dyslexia also promote systematic-intensive phonics for all students, specifically Orton-Gillingham (OG). But struggling to read is, in fact, quite common, and a long, chaotic process. Teaching reading is very complex, unique to each child, and as the International Literacy Association (ILA; 2016) clarifies, "There is no certifiably best method for teaching children who experience reading difficulty" (p. 3). Therefore, demands that all children attain some prescribed proficiency in reading by third grade are expectations that *all* children meet a *subset* of human behavior (normal). This is as senseless and unattainable as the joke about Lake Wobegon, where *all* children are above average.

No child should be invisible in schools, but pathologizing childhood behavior that is quite common because some adults have irresponsible deadlines and expectations for those children is inexcusable. *Teaching children to read needs a new normal*, one that acknowledges the power of learning and living conditions while avoiding the dangers of finding fault in any child that we can simply cure with a silver bullet.

To better understand the "science of reading" version of the reading war, Chapter 3 examines the key concepts and terms that are often misunderstood and misrepresented, perpetuating the same patterns found in each version of the reading war for far too many decades in the United States.

References

Allington, R. L. (2019, Fall). The hidden push for phonics legislation. *Tennessee Literacy Journal, 1*(1), 7–20.

Bracey, G. (2006). *Reading educational research: How to avoid getting statistically snookered.* Portsmouth, NH: Heinemann.

Collins, T. (2019, December 4). Mississippi rising? A partial explanation for its NAEP improvement is that it holds students back. *Thomas B. Fordham Institute.* Retrieved from https://fordhaminstitute.org/national/commentary/mississippi-rising-partial-explanation-its-naep-improvement-it-holds-students

Darling-Hammond, L. (1997, November). *Doing what matters most: Investing in quality teaching.* Kutstown, PA: The National Commission on Teaching and America's Future.

Davis, A. (2013). To read or not to read: Decoding synthetic phonics. *IMPACT, 2013*(20), 1–38. https://doi.org/10.1111/2048-416X.2013.12000.x

Di Carlo, M. (2010, July 14). Teachers matter, but so do words. *Albert Shanker Institute.* Retrieved from http://www.shankerinstitute.org/blog/teachers-matter-so-do-words

Ellison, K. (2015, November 4). French kids DO have ADHD. *Psychology Today.* Retrieved from https://www.psychologytoday.com/us/blog/pay-attention/201511/french-kids-do-have-adhd

Flesch, R. (1986). *Why Johnny can't read: And what you can do about it.* New York, NY: William Morrow Paperbacks.

Garan, E. M. (2001, March). Beyond smoke and mirrors: A critique of the National Reading Panel report on phonics. *Phi Delta Kappan, 82*(7), 500–506. https://doi.org/10.1177/003172170108200705

Gennetian, L. A., Sciandra, M., Sanbonmatsu, L., Ludwig, J., Katz, L. F., Duncan, G. J.,...Kessler, R. C. (2012). The long-term effects of moving to opportunity on youth outcomes. *Cityscape: A Journal of Policy Development and Research, 14*(2), 137–168.

Hanford, E. (2018, September 10). Hard words: Why aren't kids being taught to read? *APM Reports.* Retrieved from https://www.apmreports.org/story/2018/09/10/hard-words-why-american-kids-arent-being-taught-to-read

Hanford, E. (2019, December 5). There is a right way to teach reading, and Mississippi knows it. *The New York Times.* Retrieved from https://www.nytimes.com/2019/12/05/opinion/mississippi-schools-naep.html

Hughes, J. N., West, S. G., Kim, H., & Bauer, S. S. (2017, November 9). Effect of early grade retention on school completion: A prospective study. *Journal of Educational Psychology*, Advance online publication. http://dx.doi.org/10.1037/edu0000243

Human Rights Campaign. (2019). *The lies and dangers of efforts to change sexual orientation or gender identity.* Retrieved from https://www.hrc.org/resources/the-lies-and-dangers-of-reparative-therapy

International Literacy Association. (2016). *Dyslexia* [Research advisory]. Newark, DE: Author. Retrieved from http://literacyworldwide.org/docs/default-source/where-we-stand/ila-dyslexia-research-advisory.pdf

Jasper, K., Carter, C., Triscari, R., & Valesky, T. (2017, January 9). *The effects of mandated 3rd grade retention: An analysis of Florida's A+ plan.* Retrieved from https://static1.squarespace.com/static/55e6f66ae4b084d88962a8c7/t/5878c86acd0f689b626d535b/1484310635090/Executive+Summary+.pdf

Koerth-Baker, M. (2013, October 15). The not-so-hidden cause behind the A.D.H.F. epidemic. *The New York Times.* Retrieved from https://www.nytimes.com/2013/10/20/magazine/the-not-so-hidden-cause-behind-the-adhd-epidemic.html

Kozuch, E. (2017, December 15). #FlashbackFriday—Today in 1973, the APA removed homosexuality from list of a mental illnesses. *Human Rights Campaign.* Retrieved from http://www.hrc.org/blog/flashbackfriday-today-in-1973-the-apa-removed-homosexuality-from-list-of-me

Krashen, S. (2013). Access to books and time to read versus the Common Core State Standards and tests. *English Journal, 103*(2), 21–29.

Malin, J. R., & Lubienski, C. (2015). Educational expertise, advocacy, and media influence. *Education Policy Analysis Archives, 23*(6). http://dx.doi.org/10.14507/epaa.v23.1706

Miller, A. (1954). *The crucible.* New York, NY: Bantam Books.

Molnar, A. (2001, April). *The media and educational research: What we know vs. what the public hears.* Paper presented at the 2001 AERA annual meeting, Seattle, Washington. Retrieved from https://nepc.colorado.edu/sites/default/files/cerai-01-14.htm

National Conference of State Legislatures. (2019, April 16). *Third-grade reading legislation.* Retrieved from http://www.ncsl.org/research/education/third-grade-reading-legislation.aspx

National Council of Teachers of English. (2015, February 28). *Resolution on mandatory grade retention and high-stakes testing.* Urbana, IL: Author. Retrieved from http://www2.ncte.org/statement/grade-retention/

National Reading Panel. (2000a, April). *Teaching children to read: Reports of the subgroups.* Washington, DC: U.S. Department of Health and Human Services. Retrieved from https://www.nichd.nih.gov/sites/default/files/publications/pubs/nrp/Documents/report.pdf

National Reading Panel. (2000b, April). *Report of the National Reading Panel: Teaching children to read.* Washington, DC: U.S. Department of Health and Human Services. Retrieved from https://www.nichd.nih.gov/publications/pubs/nrp/smallbook

Palmer, J. (2018, December 14). Student retention: About the data. *Oklahoma Watch.* Retrieved from https://oklahomawatch.org/2018/12/14/student-retention-about-the-data/

Ponnou, S., & Gonon, F. (2017). How French media have portrayed ADHD to the lay public and to social workers. *International Journal Of Qualitative Studies on Health and Well-being, 12*(sup1). https://doi.org/10.1080/17482631.2017.1298244

The Reading First Program's Grant Application Process. (2006, September). *Final inspection report.* Washington, DC: U.S. Department of Education. Retrieved from https://www2.ed.gov/about/offices/list/oig/aireports/i13f0017.pdf

Richards, E. (2019, October 30). Despite Common Core and more testing, reading and math scores haven't budged in a decade. *USA Today.* Retrieved from https://www.usatoday.com/story/news/education/2019/10/29/national-math-reading-level-test-score-common-core-standards-phonics/2499622001/

Rose, S. (2012, August). *Third grade reading policies.* Denver, CO: Education Commission of the States. Retrieved from https://www.ecs.org/clearinghouse/01/03/47/10347.pdf

Schmidt, R., & Thomas, P. L. (2009). *21st century literacy: If we are scripted, are we literate?* Heidelberg, Germany: Springer.

Thomas, P. L. (2012). *Ignoring poverty in the U.S.: The corporate takeover of public education.* Charlotte NC: Information Age.

Thomas, P. (2013, September 12). Whatever happened to scientifically based research in education policy? *AlterNet.* Retrieved from https://www.alternet.org/2013/09/whatever-happened-scientifically-based-research-education-policy/

Thomas, P. L., & Goering, C. Z. (2016). *NEPC review: Learning about learning: What every new teacher needs to know.* Boulder, CO: National Education Policy Center. Retrieved from http://nepc.colorado.edu/thinktank/review-teacher-education

Trelease, J. (2006). *All in the family: The Bushes and the McGraws.* Retrieved from http://www.trelease-on-reading.com/whatsnu_bush-mcgraw.html

Wedge, M. (2012, March 8). Why French kids don't have ADHD. *Psychology Today.* Retrieved from https://www.psychologytoday.com/us/blog/suffer-the-children/201203/why-french-kids-dont-have-adhd

Willingham, D. (2018, October 29). Just how polarized are we about reading instruction? *Daniel Willingham—Science & Education.* Retrieved from http://www.danielwillingham.com/daniel-willingham-science-and-education-blog/just-how-polarized-are-we-about-reading-instruction

Yatvin, J. (2003). I told you so! The misinterpretation and misuse of The National Reading Panel Report. *Education Week, 22*(33), 44–45, 56. Retrieved from https://www.edweek.org/ew/articles/2003/04/30/33yatvin.h22.html

Yettick, H. (2009). *The research that reaches the public: Who produces the educational research mentioned in the News Media?* Boulder, CO: Education and the Public Interest Center Education Policy Research Unit. Retrieved from https://nepc.colorado.edu/sites/default/files/PB-Yettick-MEDIA.pdf

3

Misreading Reading

The Good, the Bad, and the Ugly

So far, I have offered a historical perspective for the reading war, followed by a careful unpacking of the current "science of reading" reading war. Here, I want to address what I believe is another central problem with any reading war: misinformation and misunderstanding key terms and concepts. This chapter also addresses the subtitle of the book, *A Primer for Parents, Policy Makers, and People Who Care,* so anyone who genuinely cares about teaching reading, children reading, or the public debate about reading and education can be better informed.

These topics have been discussed or mentioned in the previous chapters, but now I present a fuller discussion of the following: the National Reading Panel (NRP), reading programs, balanced literacy (BL), whole language (WL), phonics, scientific research, grade retention, teacher education, and teacher autonomy. With a better understanding of these essential concepts, anyone can navigate the reading war, including evaluating how the media continue to misinform and mislead (see Appendix B: "Checklist: Media Coverage of the 'Science of Reading'").

How to End the Reading War and Serve the Literacy Needs of All Students, pages 57–91
Copyright © 2020 by Information Age Publishing

The Enduring Influence of the National Reading Panel (and the "D" Word)

News articles across *Education Week*, NPR, PBS, the *New York Times*, and other mainstream outlets have praised the need for the science of reading while almost uniformly referring to the NRP as the primary or at least an exemplary research base for that "science." The NRP report has been significantly challenged by scholars of literacy and, specifically, a member of the committee, Joanne Yatvin (2002), issued a minority report while also noting that the panel included no genuine teacher of reading; Yatvin also explained that the report is inadequate and predicted accurately it would be misrepresented and misused in the following ways:

> **FALSE:** The National Reading Panel was a diverse and balanced group of reading experts.
>
> **TRUE:** Congress asked for a balanced panel, but that's not what it got...
>
> **FALSE:** The panel carried out a comprehensive analysis of the entire field of reading research.
>
> **TRUE:** Only a small fraction of the field was considered, and only a few hundred studies were actually analyzed...
>
> **FALSE:** The panel determined that there are five essentials of reading instruction.
>
> **TRUE:** Although the NRP reported positive results for five of the six instructional strategies it investigated, it never claimed that these five were the essential components of reading...
>
> **FALSE:** The panel endorsed only explicit, systematic instruction. [a]
>
> **TRUE:** Only in the phonics subgroup report is "explicit, systematic" instruction called essential...
>
> **FALSE:** The panel identified certain comprehensive commercial reading programs as being research-based, and concluded that teachers need one of these programs, or a comparable program, to teach children effectively.
>
> **TRUE:** No comprehensive reading programs were investigated by the panel. The panel had nothing to say about whether teachers need a commercial program or can develop their own...
>
> **FALSE:** The panel identified phonics as the most important component of reading instruction throughout the elementary grades.
>
> **TRUE:** The panel made no such determination...
>
> **FALSE:** The panel found that phonics should be taught to all students throughout the elementary grades.
>
> **TRUE:** The panel found no evidence to justify teaching phonics to normally progressing readers past first grade...

FALSE: The panel's findings repudiate whole language as an approach to teaching reading.
TRUE: The panel did not investigate whole language as a topic and did not draw any conclusions about it as an approach to teaching reading...
FALSE: The panel found research evidence indicating how teachers should be trained to teach reading. [a]
TRUE: The panel found no such evidence... (Yatvin, 2002)

I stand fast that even though Yatvin technically is a minority opinion, she has the greatest expertise of the panel and her clarifications and warnings have proven accurate. But there is more reason to reject the NRP report as sacrosanct guidance for how to teach reading; it was at the center of the politically corrupt Reading First scandal that exposed relationships between government officials and Open Court textbooks (The Reading First Program's Grant Application Process, 2006; Trelease, 2006).

The short version about the full picture of the NRP is that it was a politically skewed panel from the beginning, and then its process was also deeply flawed (Garan, 2001), manipulating what research was considered in order to favor a systematic-intensive phonics message that wasn't supported by the actual science of reading available then, and now. To reference the NRP report as credible is to *overstate its value*, to misrepresent not only the report but the field of teaching reading. Yet, journalists with no expertise in literacy and no background in the history of reading or teaching reading are falling prey to alluring language, "the science of reading," and fulfilling the warnings offered by Yatvin nearly two decades ago.

Finally, then, what does the NRP actually say about phonics? Here are some key findings, *flawed as they are*, from the phonics subgroup (National Reading Panel, 2000b):

Phonics instruction taught early proved much more effective than phonics instruction introduced after first grade. Mean effect sizes were kindergarten $d = 0.56$; first grade $d = 0.54$; 2nd through 6th grades $d = 0.27$. The conclusion drawn is that phonics instruction produces the biggest impact on growth in reading when it begins in kindergarten or 1st grade before children have learned to read independently. These results indicate clearly that systematic phonics instruction in kindergarten and 1st grade is highly beneficial and that children at these developmental levels are quite capable of learning phonemic and phonics concepts. (p. 2–93)

Phonics instruction produced substantial reading growth among younger children at risk of developing future reading problems. Effect sizes were $d = 0.58$ for kindergartners at risk and $d = 0.74$ for 1st graders at risk. Phonics instruction also significantly improved the reading performance of disabled readers (i.e., children with average IQs but poor reading) for whom the effect size was $d = 0.32$. These effect sizes were all statistically greater than zero. However, phonics instruction failed to exert a significant impact on the reading performance of low-achieving readers in 2nd through 6th grades (i.e., children with reading difficulties and possibly other cognitive difficulties explaining their low achievement)....

Systematic phonics instruction was most effective in improving children's ability to decode regularly spelled words ($d = 0.67$) and pseudowords ($d = 0.60$). This was expected because the central focus of systematic phonics programs is upon teaching children to apply the alphabetic system to read novel words. Systematic phonics programs also produced growth in the ability to read irregularly spelled words although the effect size was significantly lower, $d = 0.40$. This is not surprising because a decoding strategy is less helpful for reading these words. However, alphabetic knowledge is useful for establishing connections in memory that help children read irregular words they have read before. This may explain the contribution of phonics.

Systematic phonics instruction produced significantly greater growth than non-phonics instruction in younger children's reading comprehension ability ($d = 0.51$). However, the effects of systematic phonics instruction on text comprehension in readers above 1st grade were mixed. Although gains were significant for the subgroup of disabled readers ($d = 0.32$), they were not significant for the older group in general ($d = 0.12$). (p. 2–94)

One concern relates to the commonly heard call for "intensive, systematic" phonics instruction. Usually the term "intensive" is not defined, so it is not clear how much teaching is required to be considered "intensive." ...

"Does one size fit all?" Teachers may be expected to use a particular phonics program with their class, yet it quickly becomes apparent that the program suits some students better than others. (p. 2–96)

There will be some children who already know most letter-sound correspondences, some children who can even decode words, and others who have little or no letter knowledge. Should teachers proceed through the program and ignore these students? Or should they assess their students' needs and select the types and amounts of phonics suited to those needs? Although the latter is clearly preferable, this requires phonics programs that provide guidance in how to place students into flexible instructional groups and how to pace instruction. However, it is common for many phonics programs to present a fixed sequence of lessons scheduled from the beginning to the end of the school year.

Finally, it is important to emphasize that systematic phonics instruction should be integrated with other reading instruction to create a balanced reading program. Phonics instruction is never a total reading program. In 1st grade, teachers can provide controlled vocabulary texts that allow students to practice decoding, and they can also read quality literature to students to build a sense of story and to develop vocabulary and comprehension. Phonics should not become the dominant component in a reading program, neither in the amount of time devoted to it nor in the significance attached. It is important to evaluate children's reading competence in many ways, not only by their phonics skills but also by their interest in books and their ability to understand information that is read to them. By emphasizing all of the processes that contribute to growth in reading, teachers will have the best chance of making every child a reader. (p. 2–97)

An overarching final important point about the NRP is that while there may be some value in the report for careful and informed readers, as Yatvin (2002) concedes, the NRP report is in no way evidence that there is a settled science of reading. In fact, the NRP report exposes how dangerous making the claim of settled is, especially when that becomes the tool of government bureaucracy or the lever of commercial reading programs. Anyone citing the NRP must keep in mind Garan's (2001) analysis of the phonics, concluding:

> If *Teaching Children to Read* were a typical research study, published in an education journal and destined to be read only by other researchers, then I could simply end my analysis by saying that the panel's own words have established that the research base in its report on phonics is so flawed that the results do not even matter. However, as we have seen, this study has clout. It has a public relations machine behind it that has already promulgated the results throughout a very wide, very public arena as representing unbiased scientific "truth." (p. 506)

Almost 20 years ago, Garan (2001) had the same concerns as Yatvin (2002), both of which have come disturbingly true:

> The conclusions of this study as reported in the Summary have generated headlines not only in education publications, such as *Education Week* and *Reading Today*, but also in such newspapers as *USA Today*, the *Cleveland Plain Dealer*, and the *Indianapolis Star*. It is, perhaps, too late to mitigate the effects of this widely distributed, widely publicized project. However, I can hope that this analysis will provide a tool for others who will want to delve more deeply into the findings of the NRP report before accepting or rejecting it on the basis of the philosophical hot topics that the research addresses. If our instructional methods are to be dictated by research, then shouldn't that research be sound? (Garan, 2001, p. 506)

Now, we should be answering that question with a definitive "yes" even as that resists the misguided call of the science of reading.

Teaching Reading and Children: Reading Programs as "Costume Parties"

Well into my 30s and during my doctoral program, I was finally afforded the opportunity to read carefully the work of John Dewey. This late scholarship on my part is an indictment of teacher certification (see below), but it is also a window into the historical and current misinformation about the state of reading and the teaching of reading in U.S. schools. Dewey, the Father of Progressive Education, I discovered, believed that *we do not need to teach reading*; Dewey noted that reading just happened, basing this claim on his own inability to recall having been taught to read.

The first time I came across this—considering I was then and remain primarily a teacher of English—I was puzzled that Dewey could be so wrong about reading and so compelling about education in general. With time, however, I realized that my initial rejection of Dewey's belief about reading sprang from my perspective as a teacher: Teachers are predisposed to seeing themselves as change agents, as *causing* the learning of students. As an avid reader and writer, if I am honest, my perspective on reading isn't all that different from Dewey's. It is likely that Dewey and I experienced similar conditions of privilege that *allowed* something like a *natural* learning of reading, and literacy in general. And it is here that we must confront a foundational question: Why have we declared a perpetual reading crisis in the United States throughout the last century?

Progressive education and Dewey became and often remain targets of traditional claims that U.S. public education is a failure along with announcing that the United States has a reading crisis. But, as Alfie Kohn (2008) has detailed:

> Despite the fact that all schools can be located on a continuum stretching between the poles of totally progressive and totally traditional—or, actually, on a series of continuums reflecting the various components of those models—it's usually possible to visit a school and come away with a pretty clear sense of whether it can be classified as predominantly progressive. It's also possible to reach a conclusion about how many schools—or even individual classrooms—in America merit that label: damned few. The higher the grade level, the rarer such teaching tends to be, and it's not even all that prevalent at the lower grades. (Also, while it's probably true that most progressive schools are independent, most independent schools are not progressive.)

The rarity of this approach, while discouraging to some of us, is also rather significant with respect to the larger debate about education. If progressive schooling is actually quite uncommon, then it's hard to blame our problems (real or alleged) on this model. Indeed, the facts have the effect of turning the argument on its head: If students aren't learning effectively, it may be because of the persistence of traditional beliefs and practices in our nation's schools. (paras. 23–24)

As discussed in earlier chapters, Lou LaBrant's career and her scholarship represent both an accurate case for progressive approaches to teaching reading and a record of how U.S. public schools have failed the promise those practices offered.

More so than Dewey, LaBrant (1944) in her scholarship and practice represent a practical progressive pedagogy that rises above *natural* and includes *critical*: "Two adults speak of 'progressive education.' One means a school where responsibility, critical thinking, and honest expression are emphasized; the other thinks of license, lack of plans, irresponsibility. They argue fruitlessly about being 'for' or 'against' progressive education" (pp. 477–478). Dewey's claim of "natural" learning has led critics to demonizing the latter, while LaBrant's practices are grounded in the former. In reality, again as Kohn shows, neither the misapplication of a laissez-faire progressivism nor holistic, child-centered progressivism has ever characterized the learning experiences of most U.S. students, despite what the science of reading advocates claim about the failures of teaching reading.

And thus, LaBrant's arguments throughout the first half of the 20th century remain relevant. "Language behavior can not be reduced to formula," LaBrant (1947, p. 20) argued—emphasizing that literacy growth was complicated but flourished when it was child-centered and practical (e.g., in the ways many privileged children experience in their homes because one or more of the parents are *afforded* the conditions within which to foster their children's literacy). By mid-20th century, LaBrant (1949) had identified the central failure of teaching reading: "Our language programs have been set up as costume parties and not anything more basic than that" (p. 16).

In fact, many years before this observation, LaBrant (1936) confronted the failure of implementing progressive philosophy in real-world classrooms:

An Experience Curriculum in English [A Report of a Commission of the National Council of Teachers of English. W. Wilbur Hatfield, Chairman. D. Appleton—Century Company, 1935], published only a year ago, is already influencing the course of study in many schools. There is always danger in popular revision that the change may be confined to stated objectives and superficial devices, and that basic understandings may not be involved at all. A teacher eager to join the ranks of progressives recently asked the question: "How can I put the teaching of The Lady of the Lake on an experience basis in my ninth-grade class?" The question is but little less absurd than the procedures of many curriculum revisers who re-arrange old materials, add a little in- formality to class discussions and present the result as a mark of progress. We must consequently beware lest many so-called "experience curriculums" be set up without recognition of opportunity for normal, strong and complex experiences, within which language development in reading, writing, talking and listening is an integral factor. (p. 295)

Despite LaBrant's optimism above about the impact of NCTE's report, the history of reading programs in the United States remains a disappointing trail of costume parties. In fact, the history of reading instruction as little more than a masquerade was tackled by LaBrant (1931) just 5 years before, her confronting of project-based learning examined in Chapter 1. The misapplication of the project method as arts and crafts (instead of reading) is a close cousin to what passes for reading instruction today: test-prep for reading tests (instead of reading).

If LaBrant were alive today, I suspect she would express wrath for standards, the high-stakes testing, and the science of reading mantra that are the source of the reading programs bonanza now sweeping across the United States: This is once again allowing reading programs to masquerade as reading instruction—except these costume parties are incredibly costly in terms of time and public funding and detrimental to the exact students who need genuine progressive learning environments the most. Are we, then, failing reading once again?

In short, the sort of practices that we have known to be effective for better reading by students since LaBrant's career (and echoed by leading literacy experts decade after decade) simply don't sell, simply do not fit into reading programs of the neat package of the science of reading:

- Alleviate poverty and inequity so that all children live in homes that foster early reading development.
- Emphasize choice reading, not prescriptive reading programs, as essential to reading development.
- Ensure access to books, such as libraries as well as books in the home, as central to reading growth.

Thus, if genuine social and school reform focused on the above, instead of new standards, new tests, and new materials, consider the consequences: If all children entered schools as literate as most affluent children, the reading program industry would be destroyed.

Just as the market economy of the United States depends on poverty to thrive (and thus market forces will never overcome poverty), the reading program industry depends on struggling readers and thus will never seek ways to foster reading among all children. The reading program industry also feeds on any reading war, and will capitalize on the science of reading as a marketing tool.

The choice before us is to continue the masquerade that is the science of reading—one that lines the pockets of curriculum consultants, textbook and testing companies, and government bureaucrats—or to make a truly progressive commitment to both the lives and schools of all children, lives, and schools that allow learning that seems natural.

The Problem With Balanced Literacy

My summer graduate course, Foundations and Current Trends in Literacy Research and Practice, never fails at being an invigorating course for me and my students because it combines foundational topics in literacy with a never-ending series of current debates and controversies surrounding those enduring elements of teaching and learning literacy. For several years recently, my home state of South Carolina has provided ample course content because of the current reading legislation, Read to Succeed, modeled in part on Florida's reading policy and commitment to grade retention as a punitive key element in teaching reading.

Even with Read to Succeed firmly entrenched and resulting in grade retention for students, a new wave of controversy invigorated this course's topics—the media focus on the science of reading driven by advocates for students with dyslexia and the (tired) resurgence of calls for systematic phonics for all students, the newest reading war that is the focus of this book. The scapegoats in this science of reading frenzy are teacher education and balanced literacy (the younger cousin of the similarly maligned whole language). At the end of one class preceding the next day's focus on BL, a graduate student asked for a quick definition because since she was new to education and had recently experienced many interviews that asked her to define BL, she felt quite disoriented and uninformed about what it means.

I pulled up my standard paragraph from Dixie Lee Spiegel (1998) and immediately heard several other students note this isn't how they have had the term defined in their schools:

> This leads me to the following definition: A balanced approach to literacy development is a decision-making approach through which the teacher makes thoughtful choices each day about the best way to help each child become a better reader and writer. A balanced approach is not constrained by or reactive to a particular philosophy. It is responsive to new issues while maintaining what research has already shown to be effective. It is an approach that requires and frees a teacher to be a reflective decision maker and to fine tune and modify what he or she is doing each day in order to meet the needs of each child. (p. 116)

While many in literacy may debate some of the finer details of Spiegel's definition, and other definitions of WL, for example, the key point here is that BL is an effort to emphasize the professionalism of each teacher to address the needs of each student, and thus all students, instead of simply complying with state standards, implementing a required reading program, or preparing students for a high-stakes test.

As I read the daily reflections, the next class session on the readings for balanced literacy, this response, I think, is an important way to address the problem with balanced literacy (edited for some minor formatting):

> My school places a huge emphasis on balanced literacy. *However, it is presented more in terms of how much time and in what context various components of literacy should be implemented in class daily (we even have it in a pie chart)* [emphasis added]. We used to have a great deal of autonomy in the curriculum we chose in reading and writing, but our district recently adopted Lucy Calkins' Units of Study. Although Calkins desires for teachers to use her units as a framework, *it has become a way to make sure all teachers are doing the same thing* [emphasis added]. In practice we have a balanced literacy program in terms of we give students choice (although in the early grades very restricted choices), allow time for free reading, a lot of experience with literacy, small, guided reading group instruction, and explicit phonics instruction; we are doing all of this in a systematic, controlled way. I read the article about effective balanced literacy instruction and felt it did a great job in summarizing the qualities that make a teacher highly effective in the implementation of balanced literacy. But the point is...it takes a highly effective teacher, period.

> Having only been consistently teaching for five years, I also understand how incredibly challenging it is to be a masterful teacher. I feel I could have seemed that I was implementing balanced literacy proficiently in a class I had two years ago. Most of my class came from literacy rich environments and could discuss books in meaningful ways. The ones that did struggle, were inspired by their peers to take risks in reading (they made me look good). This past year, I did not have a class as a whole that loved reading. For a lot of them, it was a challenge to get them to listen to stories much less engage in meaningful conversations. The majority of them would say

they hated to read. Calkins (and my reading coach) would have me go to a first-grade unit of study and implement more basic literacy skills to scaffold, but there was no way I would be able to do this alone. The lessons are very in depth and it would have cost me more time than I had available. Also, those mini-lessons would not have appealed to the 6 or 8 students who were ready to have more comprehensive, richer discussions. Reading and literacy implementation was a struggle all year.

I also realize that it is easier within systems to quantify and package things, but you simply cannot do this with teachers and students [emphasis added]. It is easy to show learning in a quantitative way. Although my students achieved higher reading levels this year, which looks great on an SLO [Student Learning Objectives], as a teacher I know that I missed it with them. *I also realize that I can say I am doing balanced literacy, but I know it isn't truly what balanced literacy is intended to be* [emphasis added].

To open the class discussion of BL, after reading this and other reflections with similar descriptions, I explained to the class that both WL and BL are philosophies of teaching and acquiring literacy; they provide evidence-based broad concepts to guide practice, but neither was originally intended to be prescriptive programs or templates for teaching and learning.

As the response above demonstrates, however, education in practice is often overreliant on programs and less diligent about addressing philosophy or theory. In short, the problem with BL is *not* that teacher education teaches BL and not the science of reading (BL as a philosophy of literacy embraces a full and complex science of reading) and *not* that teachers do not know the science of reading but are teaching BL, but that almost all schools have adopted programs, many of which claim the label of "balanced literacy" while also breaking the foundational elements of that philosophy (see the last sentence of the response above). These reading programs (labeled "balanced literacy" or not) are primarily about addressing standards, preparing students for high-stakes tests, and imposing a prescriptive one-size-fits-all approach to teaching and learning reading; and therein is the essential flaw.

*All teachers and all students doing the same things at the same time and being held accoun*table *for following the mandated program*—this is literacy instruction in the United States, and this is the grand failure almost no one in the media or in political leadership is willing to address. For the science of reading advocates to repeatedly scapegoat BL is nothing more than a distraction because it doesn't really matter what label we assign to how teachers teach reading or how students learn reading; what matters are the expertise of teachers, the needs of students, and the teaching/learning conditions that support or inhibit effective teaching and learning. The *real* problem with

BL is too few people know what it is and as a result are failing it along with the students and teachers caught in that misguided vortex.

Nonetheless, this current reading war has as a central component of the debate a relentless campaign to discredit BL. For example, the allusion to Flesch's classic work mentioned earlier in Robert Pondiscio's (2014) "Why Johnny Won't Learn to Read" accomplishes something different than he intended:

> None of these is emphasized in balanced literacy, which leans heavily on teachers "modeling" good reading habits for children, having children choose books themselves (worthwhile or not) and kids practicing strategies such as "visualizing" or "finding the main idea." Common Core focuses kids' attention on what the text says, while balanced literacy often elicits a personal response to literature.
>
> We know for a fact that balanced literacy has had little effect on closing stubborn achievement gaps separating black and Hispanic students from their white and Asian peers. Yet it still lives.

Pondiscio's uninformed swipe at BL actually reveals that, once again, ideology trumps teacher professionalism and literacy research. The reading war Pondiscio enters is about almost everything except reading (such as his attacks on political leadership and Lucy Calkins, who has become a central target and face of BL for the science of reading advocates), but the most important lesson from this newest version of the same reading war is that if we start with what WL is, we begin to see just what those who attack BL believe. Spiegel's (1998) definition included above shows that the term "balanced literacy" is about the professional autonomy of the teacher, the wide range of research on how children acquire literacy, and honoring individual student needs (those who need direct instruction and those who do not).

Before criticizing BL as a failure, then, we must be sure that what is being practiced in the classroom does in fact conform to the guiding principles of BL (Figure 3.1).

Like WL (see the next section) BL does not reject any practice that is needed or effective, and does not prescribe practices either. When Pondiscio, Hanford, and others, then, reject BL, they reject teacher autonomy and professionalism, research-based practices in literacy, and student needs simply because they have formed a negative, and false, association with the term and not the philosophy of reading and teacher professionalism that the term embodies.

Table 1
Characteristics of a Balanced Literacy Approach

• Is built on research

• Views teachers as informed decision makers and therefore is flexible

• Is built on a comprehensive view of literacy
  – Literacy involves both reading and writing
  – Reading is not just word identification, but word identification is part of reading.
  – Readers must be able to take different stances in reading: aesthetic and efferent.
  – Writers must be able to express meaningful ideas clearly.
  – Writing is not just grammar, spelling, and punctuation, but those are all part of effective writing.
  – A comprehensive program develops lifelong readers and writers.

Figure 3.1 Characteristics of a Balanced Literacy Approach. *Source*: Spiegel, 1998, p. 117.

Progressivism and Whole Language: The Irony of Failed Education Philosophies

If you read a criticism of progressivism or WL, I suspect you are reading one of two things:

1. A misrepresentation of either so that the writer can attack the misrepresentation. Sometimes this is purposeful misrepresentation, but often the misrepresentation comes from carelessness or a lack of expertise.

2. A confusion between the genuine principles of progressivism or WL and how either has been misapplied in the real world. Both progressivism and WL are terms claimed by those who also misunderstand the terms and concepts behind them. Let me emphasize: Many people have claimed to be practicing both progressivism and WL, but in fact are not being progressive, not working under the philosophical boundaries of WL; nonetheless, since they claim those labels, many use their practices to criticize both.

Since the current reading war still references WL, I offer here not necessarily an endorsement of either progressivism or WL (although I embrace many aspects of both), but a detailing of what each represents as a context for supporting or challenging either as being effective or misguided.

Progressivism is rightly associated with John Dewey, but Deweyan progressivism never found its way into mainstream public schools in any significant way. However, distortions of Dewey's focus on project-based learning (see Chapter 1 discussion of William Heard Kilpatrick's The Project Method) have a long and illuminating history. Thus, a great resource for understanding progressivism is Lou LaBrant's 1931 challenge to misguided use of projects (see Chapter 1). LaBrant is also a solid example of a genuine Deweyan progressive. Another important aspect of progressivism is examining how the term and practices are often misrepresented as well as how rare authentic progressivism is in real-world classrooms (Kohn, 2008).

Having a historical perspective that recognizes the paradox of blaming progressivism for educational failures—progressivism has either not been implemented widely in U.S. education, or when some have claimed to be progressive, they were in fact distorting the philosophy of education—is a solid framework for understanding the same problem with blaming WL as an educational failure.

Like progressivism, WL has suffered a long history of being blamed for failure even though it has almost never been implemented in any widespread or accurate way. As detailed in Chapter 1, WL is often associated with the urban legend from the 1990s (Krashen, 2002b)—that WL failed the entire state of California as the official reading policy:

> This is not what happened. I served on the California Language Arts Framework Committee in 1987. Phonics teaching was not banned. We simply proposed that language arts should be "literature-based." This is hardly controversial. In fact, I regarded it as part of the definition of language arts. (p. 749)

Progressivism and WL, then, share some important characteristics. Both are credible and robust philosophies built on scholarship and research, but neither has found widespread or authentic practice in traditional public schooling (both likely have had much more influence and success in private settings). However, both have been repeatedly blamed for so-called failures in the exact public-school systems where neither is practiced. Nonetheless, making a case for or against either progressivism or WL would be better served if both are accurately identified.

Finally, while it is dangerous, I think, to focus on set definitions of either BL or WL—reducing them to prescriptions in the same way as reading and phonics programs—Krashen (2002a) explains about WL:

> The Comprehension Hypothesis claims that we learn to read by understanding messages on the page; we "learn to read by reading" (Goodman, 1982; Smith, 1994). Reading pedagogy, according to the Comprehension Hypothesis, focuses on providing students with interesting, comprehensible texts,

and the job of the teacher is to help children read these texts, that is, help make them comprehensible. The direct teaching of "skills" is helpful only when it makes texts more comprehensible.

The Comprehension Hypothesis also claims that reading is the source of much of our vocabulary knowledge, writing style, advanced grammatical competence, and spelling. It is also the source of most of our knowledge of phonics. . . .

The term "whole language" does not refer only to providing interesting comprehensible texts and helping children understand less comprehensible texts. It involves instilling a love of literature, problem-solving and critical thinking, collaboration, authenticity, personalized learning, and much more (Goodman, Bird, & Goodman, 1991). In terms of the process of literacy development, however, the Comprehension Hypothesis is a central part of whole language.

WL tends to emphasize comprehension in whole and complex language experiences while advocates of systematic-intensive phonics believe literacy skills are sequential and must be built from the smallest elements of expression to the whole.

Hooked on Phonics Redux

But what about phonics? As Krashen (2002b) explains in his careful detailing of what truly happened in California in the 1980s and 1990s, phonics was not banned by WL being implemented, but the accurate evidence on phonics is much different than the science of reading argument presents:

Frank Smith has argued that some conscious knowledge of sound/spelling correspondences can help make texts comprehensible. However, there are severe limits on how much phonics can be taught directly: the rules are complex and have numerous exceptions. Smith argues that most of our knowledge of phonics is the result of reading, not the cause. (p. 751)

Systematic-intensive phonics, direct and isolated grammar instruction, vocabulary instruction—all of these are fundamental flaws in seeing the need to teach skills common in high proficiency literacy up front, to cause literacy; but a great deal of evidence suggest that whole experiences with reading and writing cause those skills to be prominent, as Krashen notes.

Yet, the overstated importance of systematic-intensive phonics is a very compelling argument. For example, the commercial reading program Hooked on Phonics, with iconic over-the-top commercials for those of us of a certain generation, had to abandon those ads in 1994:

> Under an agreement disclosed this week between the makers of the reading program Hooked on Phonics and the Federal Trade Commission, the manufacturer must abandon its advertising campaign or conduct far more research into the program's effectiveness–and disclose any evidence of failure. (Nathans, 1994, para. 1)

Anyone paying even slight attention to current media fascination with the science of reading and dyslexia may benefit from revisiting the problem with Hooked on Phonics and their outlandish claims, as Nathans (1994) adds:

> Orange County-based Gateway Educational Products, maker of Hooked on Phonics, agreed to a settlement that bars the parent company from making unsubstantiated claims about the program's ability to teach people to read. The settlement, which was signed Aug. 29, was made public Wednesday by the commission.
>
> The FTC had charged that Gateway was making sweeping, unproven promises that the program could teach anyone to read, regardless of their limitations. Gateway admitted no wrongdoing in the settlement, and will pay no penalty, said Christian S. White, acting director of the commission's bureau of consumer protection.
>
> "They offered a one-size-fits-all solution—you have reading problems, this is the product," White said. "Gateway's evidence just doesn't back up these broad, sweeping claims."
>
> The claims, according to the commission, included statements that Hooked on Phonics can teach even those with reading problems, such as dyslexia; that the product improves users' reading levels and classroom grades significantly; that it can teach reading at home, without a tutor; that it teaches comprehension of the meaning of words, and that it has helped almost 1 million people learn to read at home.
>
> The commission also said that testimonials by people who have taken the program are used misleadingly in commercials and do not prove that their experiences were typical of the average user, which is a violation of federal law. (paras. 2–6)

Although this happened 25+ years ago, currently driven by overzealous dyslexia advocacy, the mainstream media is promoting essentially the same misguided and overstated arguments about teaching reading grounded in the science of reading as code for systematic-intensive phonics for all students (see above for the more limited view of phonics included in the NRP).

The Wrong "Scientific" for Education

The release of National Assessment of Educational Progress (NAEP) 2019 scores in math and reading, announced as an "emergency" (Camera, 2019b) and "devastating" (Camera, 2019a) has thrown gasoline on the rhetorical fire that has already been sweeping across media—a call for "scientific" research to save public education in the United States:

- Schools Should Follow the 'Science of Reading,' Say National Education Groups (Schwartz, 2019b).
- Scientific Evidence on How to teach Writing Is Slim (Barshay, 2019).
- We Must Raise the Bar for Evidence in Education (Robinson & Rogers, 2019).

While the media and the public seem historically (see Chapter 1) and currently convinced by the term "scientific," there is a significant irony to the lack of scientific evidence backing claims about the *causes* of NAEP scores; for example, as I have noted in Chapter 2, some have rushed to argue that intensive-phonics instruction and grade-retention legislation have caused Mississippi's NAEP reading gains while many have used 2019 NAEP scores to declare the entire accountability era a failure.

Yet, none of these claims have the necessary scientific evidence to justify any of these arguments. There simply has not been the time or the efforts to construct scientific studies (experimental or quasi-experimental) to identify causal factors in NAEP score changes. Another problem with the rhetoric of "scientific" is that coinciding with that advocacy are some very disturbing contradictory realities:

- hasty speculation creating an anti-scientific environment for discussing education: "Screen Time Up as Reading Scores Drop. Is There a Link?" (Sparks, 2019a);
- reports implying scientific rigor but failing to implement that rigor: "In EdReports' First Review of Early-Reading Programs, No Materials Make the Grade" (Schwartz, 2019a); and
- aggressively anti-scientific education legislation: "Ohio House passes bill allowing student answers to be scientifically wrong due to religion" (WKRC Staff, 2019).

And let's not forget that for at least two decades, "scientific" has been central to No Child Left Behind (U.S. Department of Education, 2002) and the Common Core (Marchitello & Wilhelm, 2014)—both of which were championed as mechanisms for *finally* bringing education into a new era of evidence-based practices. The argument for Common Core sounds eerily similar to the arguments for the science of reading, in fact, as Marchitello and Wilhelm (2014) explain:

> Recognizing that the previous patchwork system did not work, . . . the Common Core is grounded in the latest cognitive science regarding how students learn. For this reason, there is a preponderance of evidence that strongly suggests the Common Core will improve the quality of education for all students. . . .
>
> Unlike prior state standards, the Common Core sets uniform expectations that are grounded in the knowledge and skills every child needs to be successful after high school. Decades of research about how students learn and the best practices for teaching challenging content are embedded directly into the standards. (paras. 2, 4)

We must wonder: If "scientific" is the answer to our educational failures, what has happened over the past 20 years of "scientific" being legislated into education, resulting in everyone continuing to claim that the sky is falling because 2019 NAEP scores are down from 2017 as well as relatively flat since the early 1990s (30 of the 40 years spanning accountability)?

First, there is the problem of definition. "Scientific" is often shorthand for a very narrow type of quantitative research, experimental and quasi-experimental research that is the gold standard of pharmaceutical and medical research. To meet this standard of "scientific," then, research in education would have to include random-sample populations of students and a control group (students not experiencing whatever is being studied) in order to draw causal relationships and generalize. This process is incredibly expensive in terms of funding and time. As I noted above, for example, no one has had the time to conduct "scientific" research on 2019 NAEP data so making causal claims of any kind for why NAEP scores dropped is necessarily *not* "scientific."

But there is a second, and larger, problem with calling for "scientific" research in education. This narrow form of "scientific" is simply wrong for education. Experimental and quasi-experimental research seeks to identify *causal generalizations*. In other words, if we divide all students into a bell-shaped curve with five segments, the meaty center segment would be where the generalization from a study has the greatest effectiveness. The adjacent two outer segments would show some decreasing degrees of effectiveness, leaving the two extreme segments at the far ends of the curve likely showing little or no effectiveness (these students, however, could have learned under instruction not shown as generally effective).

In real classrooms, teachers are not serving a random sampling of students, and there are no controls to assure that some factors are not causing different outcomes for students even when the instructional practice has been shown by scientific research to be effective. No matter the science behind instruction, sick, hungry, or bullied students will not be able to learn.

The truth is, in education, scientific studies are nearly impossible to conduct, may be ethically inappropriate to implement with children, are often overly burdensome in terms of expense and time, and are ultimately not practical for the needs of real teachers and students in real classrooms—where teaching and learning are messy, unpredictable, and impacted by dozens of factors beyond the control of teachers or students. Frankly, nothing works for all students, and a generalization can be of no use to a particular student with an outlier need.

If there is any causal relationship between how we teach and how students learn, it is a cumbersome matrix of factors that has been mostly unexamined, especially by "scientific" methods. And often, history is a better avenue than science. The 21st century has not been the only era calling for "science" in educational practice. John Dewey's progressivism of the early 20th century was also characterized by a call for scientific practice. Recall from Chapter 1, LaBrant (1947) called repeatedly for closing the "gap" between research and practice, but she also balked at reading and writing programs—singular approaches to teaching all students literacy.

While progressive education and Dewey are often demonized and blamed for educational failure by the mid-20th century (see above), the truth is that progressive calls for a broader "scientific" has never been widely embraced in the United States. Today, however, we should be skeptical of the narrow and flawed call for "scientific" and embrace instead that progressive "scientific." For Dewey, the teacher must simultaneously teach and conduct research—what eventually would be called *action research* and what very much fits into the parameters of BL. To teach, for progressives, is to constantly gather evidence of learning from students in order to drive instruction; in this context, "science" means that each student receives the instruction they demonstrate a need for and that produces some outcomes of effectiveness.

In an elementary reading class, some students may be working in read-aloud groups while others are receiving direct phonics instruction, and even others are sitting in book clubs reading picture books by choice. None of them, however, would be doing test-prep worksheets or computer-based programs. The current demand for "scientific" seems to embrace the false assumption that with the right body of research we can identify the single approach for all students to succeed. Human learning, however, is as varied as there are humans.

This is a key problem with the current "science of reading" reading war that calls for all students to receive systematic-intensive phonics, purportedly because scientific research calls for such. The science of reading narrative also rejects and demonizes BL as *not* "scientific." We arrive then back at the problem of definition. Science of reading advocacy is trapped in too narrow a definition of "scientific" that is fundamentally wrong for educating every student. Ironically, again, BL is a *philosophy of literacy* (not a program) that implements Deweyan progressive "scientific"; *each student receives the reading instruction they need based on the evidence of learning the teacher gathers from previous instruction, evidence used to guide future instruction.*

Systematic-intensive phonics for all begins with a fixed mandate regardless of student ability or need; BL starts with the evidence of the student. If we are going to argue for "scientific" education in the United States, we would be wise to change the definition, expand the evidence, and tailor our instruction to the needs of our students and not the propagandizing of a few zealots.

For two decades at least, the United States has been chasing the wrong "scientific" as a distraction from the real guiding principle, efficiency. Reducing math and reading to discrete skills and testing those skills as evidence for complex human behaviors are as misleading as arguing that "scientific" research will save education. Teachers as daily, patient researchers charged with teaching each student as that student needs—that is the better "scientific" even as it is much messier and less predictable.

South Carolina Fails Students Still: More on Grade Retention and Misreading Literacy

Before the "science of reading" slogan spread through mainstream media, many states were already adopting third-grade retention policies based on reading test scores. Despite decades of research showing grade retention is overwhelmingly harmful with very few and often short-term positive consequences (Hughes, West, Kim, & Bauer, 2017; Jasper, Carter, Triscari, & Valesky, 2017; National Council of Teachers of English, 2015), many politicians have embraced both an overstated belief in reading on grade-level in third grade and the effectiveness of grade retention. "But their remedies do not cure the disease: they merely prolong it," wrote Oscar Wilde (1891, para. 2). "Indeed, their remedies are part of the disease."

Bells will certainly continue to signal class changes in public schools all across South Carolina this fall, but there is a much more serious (and unwarranted) bell of doom for many third-graders because of South Carolina's punitive Read to Succeed legislation, typical of this legislation across the United States (Hyde, 2017). Once again, literacy policy often fails to address valid literacy practices or to acknowledge that literacy proficiency is strongly correlated with systemic conditions beyond the walls of the school or the control of teachers.

Worksheets on literacy skills, test-prep for state assessments of reading and writing, linking teacher evaluations to students' test scores, and retaining children are simply not only flawed literacy policies, but also *negative influences* on children's literacy and academic achievement. And decades of creating ever-new standards and then purchasing ever-new reading textbooks and programs have utterly failed children and literacy.

For about a century, in fact, we have known what is needed to help students develop literacy—but the political will remains lacking. A robust literacy strategy for schools should include instead of retention and testing the following:

- addressing access to books in all children's homes;
- insuring access to books in all children's schools;
- providing all students ample and extended time in class to read by choice;
- guaranteeing every student fully informed literacy instruction based on each student's demonstrated literacy needs (not the prescriptions of literacy programs); and
- discontinuing the standards and testing disaster dominating schools and classrooms by providing teachers the materials, time, and *professional autonomy* to teach literacy in evidence-based ways.

Just as education policy ignores a rich and diverse research base, political leaders and the public refuse to address how public policy directly and indirectly impacts student achievement; the following would create higher student achievement and literacy:

- eradicating food deserts and ensuring food security,
- providing universal health care to children and families with children, and
- creating job security for families with children.

Finally, we must acknowledge that grade retention fulfills a cultural negative attitude about children and people in poverty among the United States public—one grounded in individual blame and punishment. But decades of research has shown (yes, even with the failed Florida policy that serves as a template for many states such as South Carolina) that grade retention may raise test scores short term, but that gain disappears in a few years and the many negative consequences of retention remain (Jasper, Carter, Triscari, & Valesky, 2017).

As the National Council of Teachers of English detail in their position statement on grade retention and high-stakes testing, grade retention fails in the following ways:

- retaining students who have not met proficiency levels with the intent of repeating instruction is punitive, socially inappropriate, and educationally ineffective;
- basing retention on high-stakes tests will disproportionately and negatively impact children of color, impoverished children, English language learners, and special needs students; and
- retaining students is strongly correlated with behavior problems and increased drop-out rates. (National Council of Teachers of English, 2015)

Of course, all children need and deserve rich and rewarding literacy experiences and growth, but third-grade literacy is both a manufactured metric by textbook and testing companies and a misleading emergency (see below).

Grade retention and skills- and standards-based literacy instruction and testing have failed and continue to fail horribly the students who need authentic literacy instruction the most—Black and Brown children, English language learners (who may need a *decade* to acquire a second language), students in poverty, and special needs students. These populations are a significant portion of the students served in states where public schools typically have low reading test scores; hateful and misguided policies are created and tolerated by a more White and affluent political leadership and public who have racist and classist biases against "other people's children."

In fact, failed literacy policy in South Carolina can be linked directly to how the United States demonizes and fails the impoverished:

> It all starts with the psychology concept known as the "fundamental attribution error." This is a natural tendency to see the behavior of others as being determined by their character—while excusing our own behavior based on circumstances.

For example, if an unexpected medical emergency bankrupts you, you view yourself as a victim of bad fortune—while seeing other bankruptcy court clients as spendthrifts who carelessly had too many lattes. Or, if you're unemployed, you recognize the hard effort you put into seeking work—but view others in the same situation as useless slackers. Their history and circumstances are invisible from your perspective. (Szalavitz, 2017, paras. 4–5)

Students struggling to read are viewed as lacking or broken, in need of repair and/or punishment to correct.

If you think this is harsh, compare how mostly White and more affluent students learn literacy in advanced and gifted classes in public schools (a dirty little secret about how we have maintained segregation) and most private schools. Like No Child Left Behind and Every Student Succeeds Act, Read to Succeed and similar reading programs across the United States use Orwellian names for a disturbing way to view, treat, and teach children.

In South Carolina, the state implemented Read to Succeed, a reading policy built in part on the Florida formula (Just Read, Florida!) that has a great deal of political support but has been unmasked as yet another misleading education "miracle" that wasn't (Jasper, Carter, Triscari, & Valesky, 2017). The most flawed aspect of Read to Succeed is that it mimics Florida's third-grade retention policy that retains third graders based on standardized test scores. In our current era that suggests all states should be embracing the science of reading, then, how can any state justify grade retention, unsupported by research?

South Carolina tried to give the appearance that the legislation was research-based and comprehensive, yet the Read to Succeed act and the EOC support actually represent what Matthew Di Carlo (2014) has identified as a central problem with policy built on a misuse of data:

> The recent release of the National Assessment of Educational Progress (NAEP) and the companion Trial Urban District Assessment (TUDA) was predictably exploited by advocates to argue for their policy preferences. This is a blatant misuse of the data for many reasons that I have discussed here many times before, and I will not repeat them. . . . (para. 1)

> But they are not policy evidence. Period. . . . (para. 8)

> But, as I've said before, there's a very large group of us out here who are willing to applaud any high-level leader who refuses to misuse evidence, whether or not we happen to agree with their substantive policy positions. I'm sure there are leaders like that out there, and I wish they were more visible. (para. 10)

In the exact same way as DiCarlo details above about misusing NAEP data for political gain, Read to Succeed grew out of a flawed process even as it was promoted as research-based.

For example, when endorsing Read to Succeed, the EOC cited *only four sources*, one of which, Greene and Winters, has been reviewed, concluding: "The report reviewed here concludes that Florida's recently instituted policy of test-based retention has helped academically struggling elementary school students improve their reading. According to the review, the report overstates the effect of retention on student achievement" (Briggs, 2006, p. 1).

Further, advocacy for Read to Succeed failed to identify a strong body of research that refutes the claims made about the Florida formula and a 4-decades body of research that rejects grade retention. Reading problems are not primarily in-school problems. Reading and all literacy problems are overwhelmingly reflections of larger social problems related to inequity and poverty. Reading and literacy solutions, then, are unlikely to be found in legislation and clever program names—especially when those policies are built on partial and politically manipulated evidence, and especially when those names serve to mislead.

Beware Grade-Level Reading and the Cult of Proficiency

Few issues in education seem more important or more universally embraced (from so-called progressive educators to right-wing politicians such as Jeb Bush) than the need to have all children reading on grade level—specifically by that magical third grade:

> Five years ago, communities across the country formed a network aimed at getting more of their students reading proficiently by the end of 3rd grade. States, cities, counties, nonprofit organizations, and foundations in 168 communities, spread across 41 states and the District of Columbia, are now a part of that initiative, the Campaign for Grade-Level Reading. (Gewertz, 2015, para. 1)

However, advocating that all students must read at grade level—often labeled as "reading proficiency"—rarely acknowledges the basic problems with those goals: identifying text by a formula claiming "grade level" and then identifying children as readers by association with those readability formulas.

For example, a text, as identified by a formula, is a fifth-grade text, and thus children who can "read" that text independently are at the fifth-grade reading level. While all this seems quite scientific and efficient, I must suggest caution and even skepticism about the sort of technocratic practice that daily ruins children as readers, under-prepares children as literate and autonomous humans, and further erodes literacy as mostly *te*stable literacy. So who does this grade-level reading and proficiency benefit?

First, let's consider what anyone means by "reading." For the sake of discussion, this is oversimplified, but I think, not distorting to the point of misleading. Reading may be essentially *decoding*, pronouncing words, phrases, and clauses with enough fluency to give the impression of understanding. Reading may be *comprehension*, strategies, and then behaviors or artifacts by a reader that mostly represent (usually in different and fewer words) an accurate or mostly accurate, but unqualified, restating of the original text. But reading may also (I would add *should*) be *critical literacy*, the *investigating* of text that moves beyond comprehension and places both text and "meaning" in the dynamic of reader, writer, and text (Rosenblatt, 2005) as well as how that text is bound by issues of power while also working against the boundaries of power, history, and the limitations of language.

Typically, however, grade-level reading and proficiency is reduced to decoding and/or comprehension, promoting the argument that all meaning is *in the text only* (a concept promoted by Common Core most recently). This narrow view of text and reading (and readers) serves authoritarian approaches to teaching and mechanistic structures of testing, and more broadly, reducing text and reading to mere matters of skills serves mostly goals of surveillance and control.

Consider first the scientific attraction in formulas that masks the arbitrary nature of any formula; in other words, whoever has the power to create the formula controls what counts. Plug "The Red Wheelbarrow" by William Carlos Williams (1962) into a readability calculator (Microsoft Word can do this, for example)—first in its poetic format of lines and stanzas, and then as a grammatical sentence. As a poem, apparently, the text is about fourth grade, but as a sentence, nearly ninth grade. The problem is that readability formulas and claims of "grade level" are entirely the function of the limitations of math (the necessity to quantify and then the byproduct of honoring only that which can be quantified)—counting word syllables, number of words in sentences. See, for example, the Flesch-Kincaid readability formula:

$$206.835 - 1.015\left(\frac{\text{total words}}{\text{total sentences}}\right) - 84.6\left(\frac{\text{total syllables}}{\text{total words}}\right)$$

Reducing text to numbers and reducing students to numbers—both perpetuate a static and thus false view of text and reading. "Meaning" is not static, but shifting, contextual, and more discussion or debate than pronouncement. "The Red Wheelbarrow" (Williams, 1962) is really "easy" to read, both aloud and to comprehend. But readability formulas address nothing about genre or form, nothing about the rich intent of the writer (for example, poetry often presents only a small fraction of the larger context), nothing about all that that *various* readers bring to the text, schema mentioned in Chapter 2. And to the last point, when we confront reading on grade level or reading proficiency, we must begin to unpack *how* and *why* any reader is investigating a text.

For example, we can take a children's picture book—which by all technical matters is at primary or elementary reading grade level—and add complex lenses of analysis, rendering the same text extremely complex—with a meaning that is expanding instead of static and singular. Meaning shifts depending on the reader being a child or an adult. Text complexity, readers' grade level, and concurrent measurements such as months or years of learning are the distractions of technocrats: "It is a tale/Told by an idiot, full of sound and fury,/Signifying nothing" (*The Tragedy of Macbeth*, 5, 5).

Focusing on grade-level reading and proficiency, then, benefit politicians, textbook companies, and the exploding testing industry. But not children, not literacy, and not democracy. Leveled books, labeled children, and warped education policy (grade retention based on high-stakes testing) destroy reading and the children the science of reading advocates claim to be serving. Thus, there is simply no reading crisis and no urgency to have students on grade level, by third or any grade. The cult of proficiency and grade-level reading is simply the lingering "cult of efficiency" that plagues formal education in the United States—quantification for quantification's sake, children and literacy be damned (Callahan, 1962).

Educational Accountability and the Science of Scapegoating the Powerless: Teacher Education

Several years ago when I submitted an op-ed to the largest newspaper in my home state of South Carolina, the editor rejected the historical timeline I was using for state standards and testing, specifically arguing that accountability had begun in the late 1990s and not in the early 1980s as I noted. Here's the interesting part.

I began teaching in South Carolina in the fall of 1984, the first year of major education reform under then-governor Richard Riley. That reform included a significant teacher pay raise, extended days of working for teachers, and the standards-testing regime that would become normal for all public education across the United States. In fact, South Carolina's accountability legislation dates back to the late 1970s (I sent her online links to all this).

As a beginning teacher, the only public schooling I ever knew was teaching to standards and high-stakes tests by identifying standards on my lesson plans and implementing benchmark assessments throughout the academic year to document I was teaching what was mandated to address low student tests scores. State testing, including punitive exit exams, pervaded everything about being an English teacher then. Yet, an editor, herself a career journalist, was quick to assume my expertise as a classroom practitioner and then college professor of education was incorrect. This is a snapshot of how mainstream media interact with education as a topic and educators (both classroom K–12 teachers and teacher educators) as professionals.

I am reminded of that experience over and over in fact as I read media coverage of education. Take this, for example, from *Education Week*, "Want Teachers to Motivate Their Students? Teach Them How" (Sparks, 2019b), which has the thesis:

> Most teachers intrinsically understand the need to motivate their students, experts say, but teaching on intuition alone can lead to missteps in student engagement.
>
> A study released in May by the Mindset Scholars Network, a collaborative of researchers who study student motivation, found most teacher education programs nationwide do not include explicit training for teachers on *the science of how to motivate students* [emphasis added]. (paras. 1–2)

Two key elements of this article stand out: The new scapegoat in proclaiming education a failure is teacher education and the go-to failure is always about a lack of "science" in teacher education.

This article on motivation is following a media template well-worn recently that students in the United States can't read because teachers are not taught the science of reading in their teacher education programs. Scapegoating teacher education has many flaws, and my experience and expertise as a teacher educator for almost two decades, following almost two decades as a classroom teacher, inform my understanding of how finding scapegoats for educational failure during the accountability era is fool's gold. How has the accountability era gone in terms of how accountability policies match who is being accountable as well as how much power they have, then?

In the 1980s and 1990s, the accountability mechanisms focused on holding students accountable (such as exit exams that were gatekeepers for graduation) and schools accountable (student test scores often translated into school rankings or grades, designating schools as "failing," for example).

Keep in mind that students had no power in that process, and that schools had to implement the standards that were politically designed and mandated, again outside the power dynamics of those mandates being determined.

With No Child Left Behind came the false political claims of the Texas Miracle; the accountability era was greatly accelerated, including a creeping sense that the process wasn't improving education but it was punishing students (lower graduation rates due to exit exams) and demonizing schools (most high-poverty and high-racial minority schools were labeled as "failing"). By the administration of Barack Obama, with education policy under another false narrative (the Chicago Miracle) and false ambassador with no background in education other than appointments (Arne Duncan), the scapegoating took a turn—the problem, went the new message, was "bad" teachers (Bessie, 2010) and the solution was no longer holding students or schools accountable for test scores but those teachers (the era of value-added methods [VAM] of teacher evaluation).

As some have noted and documented, teacher-bashing increased and then prompted a backlash (see magazine covers from *Time* for a great series of artifacts on this [Strauss, 2018]); VAM proved to be a flawed process for accountability also, suggesting that maybe teachers were not the problem after all. With the scapegoat role now vacant, the media have discovered a new target, teacher education. Let's here recognize that once again the power context is way off in who is determining the accountability and who is being held accountable. *For the most part, teachers and teacher educators are relatively powerless professionals who are mandated to implement standards and assessments that they do not create and often do not endorse as valid.*

Now consider another really important reason accountability in education is deeply flawed: The constant misguided scapegoating of powerless stakeholders in formal teaching and learning is a distraction from the actual sources for educational challenges. Decades of research from educators and education scholars have detailed that out-of-school factors overwhelmingly determine measurable student outcomes, some estimates as high as 80+% and most scholars agreeing on 60%. Teacher quality's impact on measurable student achievement has been identified repeatedly as only about 10–15% (Di Carlo, 2010).

Yet, the entire accountability era since the early 1980s has focused on in-school reforms only (scapegoating students, schools, teachers, and now teacher education), while embracing harsh approaches such as "no excuses" practices that argue teachers fail students with the "soft bigotry of low expectations" and students fail because they lack "grit" or a growth mindset. Some advocates for reform such as the Schott Foundation and the

National Education Policy Center have doggedly argued for social context reform, addressing socioeconomic reform first and then reforming education along equity (not accountability) lines next, or concurrently (Thomas, Porfilio, Gorlewski, & Carr, 2014). Scholars have also demonstrated that "grit" and growth mindset have racist and classist groundings that are harmful (Wormeli, 2018). Yet those positions have been demonized and marginalized for decades.

So imagine my surprise when, first, the tide shifted on teacher bashing and then these articles suddenly appear in mainstream media: "Better Schools Won't Fix America," *The Atlantic* (Hanauer, 2019); "The Harsh Discipline of No-Excuses Charter Schools: Is It Worth the Promise?" *Education Week* (Golann & Debs, 2019); and "Unchartered Territory: 2020 Democrats Back Away From Charter Schools," *MSN* (Sarlin & Thompson, 2019). The media and journalists as generalists seem deeply resistant to learning a lesson they create over and over, and the current focus on the science of reading to blame teachers and teacher educators will once again soon to be as misguided as promoting in-school only reform, no-excuses charter policies, and charter schools in general.

Take for another example Karin Wulf's (2019) examination of Naomi Wolff and Cokie Roberts; Wulf herself is a historian:

> It's been a tough few weeks for amateur history. First, journalist Naomi Wolf discovered on live radio that she had misinterpreted key historical terms in her new book, "Outrage," leading her to draw the wrong conclusions. A week later, journalist Cokie Roberts, too, got a quick smackdown when she claimed on NPR that she couldn't find any incidence of abortion advertised in 19th century newspapers, a claim quickly disproved by historians.
>
> *Wolf and Roberts fell victim to a myth widely shared with the American public: that anyone can do history* [emphasis added]. Whether it's diving into genealogy or digging through the vast troves of digital archives now online, the public has an easy way into the world of the past. And why would they imagine it takes any special training? After all, the best-selling history books are almost always written by non-historians, from conservative commentators like Bill O'Reilly to journalists like Wolf and Roberts. (paras. 1–2)

As Wulf argues about history, with education, experience and expertise also matter.

So as I challenge the misguided science of reading reading war, writing over and over that the media are getting reading wrong, that scapegoating teacher education is missing the real problem, I wonder: How many years will it take until I see articles "discovering" these facts as if no one with experience and expertise ever raised the issue?

Pre-Service Teacher Education vs. the World

Far too many journalists and politicians simultaneously *overstate* teacher impact on student outcomes while *ignoring* that teachers in the United States have very little professional autonomy. As stated above, teacher quality contributes to only about 10–15% of measurable student achievement, much less than out-of-school factors accounting for about 60% or more of those test scores. Yet, what is also important to emphasize is that teacher practices in public schools are highly regulated, increasingly so over the past 30 years of accountability driven by standards and high-stakes testing.

Teacher professional autonomy has been nearly absent in the United States over the last century-plus—likely since it is seen as a woman's profession—but current in-service teachers will attest that their practices are significantly restrained by state mandates and schools' policies anchored to state standards and a wide assortment of high-stakes tests (from state accountability to the SAT/ACT and Advanced Placement as well as International Baccalaureate). Part of the reason I resist the inherent teacher-blaming in mainstream media rests on my own experiences as a teacher educator of English teachers for almost two decades. My journey to teacher education began as adjunct teaching in local colleges throughout the 1990s, culminating with two wonderful years as the co-lead instruction in the Spartanburg Writing Project (SWP), an affiliate of the National Writing Project.

Once I became a full-time teacher educator, I had to anticipate a recurring refrain from the wonderful young people I was helping move into the field of teaching English; they nearly all said they valued what I had taught them about best practices in teaching reading and writing, but they were not able to implement most of those practices once they secured a job teaching. *So here is the dirty little secret of education blame in the United States: We simultaneously want to hold teachers accountable for student achievement even though we know teacher quality is a small percentage of those measurable outcomes and even though teachers are often implementing practices that are not supported by research but by mandate.*

Ultimately, there is a type of education reform that has never truly been implemented in the United States—seeking ways to increase teacher professional autonomy (Will, 2017). As a former K–12 educator who moved to higher education, I can attest that professional autonomy is one of the most powerful aspects of university teaching; we are hired for our expertise and then given the respect we deserve for behaving as professionals in our classrooms. There is much about teacher certification as well as in-service teaching that deserves attention and reform, but currently, the discourse around teacher blame and why students (and schools) fail completely ignores the key cause behind criticisms of education: accountability driven by standards and high-stakes tests, which is all folded into federal and state legislation. Both teacher education and in-service teacher practices would be exponentially improved by teacher educator and teacher autonomy—and then we would find a much more valid context for holding both accountable.

*   *   *

The "science of reading" reading war represents not only similar patterns about reading and literacy found in previous versions of the reading war but also a pattern of misinformation in the public debates. This chapter has addressed some of those key concepts and terms, placing them in context so that anyone entering this debate, either as an observer or participant, can contribute more accurately to what is actually being debated—how to improve the reading lives of all students in the United States.

The heaviest lifting of this book comes next in Chapter 4, where I will offer "How to End the Reading Qar and Serve the Literacy Needs of All Students."

References

Barshay, J. (2019, November 4). Scientific evidence on how to teach writing is slim. *The Hechinger Report.* Retrieved from https://hechingerreport.org/scientific-evidence-on-how-to-teach-writing-is-slim/

Bessie, A. (2010, October 15). The myth of the bad teacher. *Truthout.* Retrieved from https://truthout.org/articles/the-myth-of-the-bad-teacher/

Briggs, D. (2006). *Review: Getting farther ahead by staying behind: A second-year evaluation of Florida's Policy to end social promotion.* Boulder, CO: Education and the Public Interest Center & Education Policy Research Unit. Retrieved from http://epicpolicy.org/thinktank/review-getting-farther-ahead-staying-behind-a-second-year-evaluation-floridas-policy-end-s

Callahan, R. E. (1962). *Education and the cult of efficiency: A study of the social forces that have shaped the administration of the public schools.* Chicago, IL: The University of Chicago Press.

Camera, L. (2019a, October 30). DeVos bemoans 'devastating' NAEP scores, pushes for 'education freedom.' *U.S. News and World Report.* Retrieved from https://www.usnews.com/news/education-news/articles/2019-10-30/devos-bemoans-devastating-naep-scores-pushes-for-education-freedom

Camera, L. (2019b, November 12). National reading emergency: Educators sound the alarm. *U.S. News and World Report.* Retrieved from https://www

.usnews.com/news/education-news/articles/2019-11-12/national
-reading-emergency-educators-sound-the-alarm

Di Carlo, M. (2010, July 14) Teachers matter, but so do words. *Albert Shanker Institute.* Retrieved from http://www.shankerinstitute.org/blog/teachers
-matter-so-do-words

Di Carlo, M. (2014, February 19). Select your conclusions, apply data. *Albert Shanker Institute.* Retrieved from http://www.shankerinstitute.org/blog/
select-your-conclusions-apply-data

Garan, E.M. (2001, March). Beyond smoke and mirrors: A critique of the National Reading Panel report on phonics. *Phi Delta Kappan, 82*(7), 500–506. https://doi.org/10.1177/003172170108200705

Gewertz, C. (2015, May 11). Push for grade-level reading takes many forms. *Education Week.* Retrieved from https://www.edweek.org/ew/articles/
2015/05/13/push-for-grade-level-reading-takes-many-forms.html

Golann, J., & Debs, M. (2019, June 9). The harsh discipline of no-excuses charter schools: Is it worth the promise? *Education Week.* Retrieved from https://www.edweek.org/ew/articles/2019/06/09/the-harsh-discipline
-of-no-excuses-charter-schools.html

Hanauer, N. (2019, July). Better schools won't fix America. *The Atlantic.* Retrieved from https://www.theatlantic.com/magazine/archive/2019/07/
education-isnt-enough/590611/

Hughes, J. N., West, S. G., Kim, H., & Bauer, S. S. (2017, November 9). Effect of early grade retention on school completion: A prospective study. *Journal of Educational Psychology.* Advance online publication. http://dx.doi
.org/10.1037/edu0000243

Hyde, P. (2017, July 6). Furman professor: SC retention policy 'a disaster.' *The Greenville News.* Retrieved from https://www.greenvilleonline.com/story/
news/2017/07/06/students/451588001/

Jasper, K., Carter, C., Triscari, R., & Valesky, T. (2017, January 9). *The effects of mandated 3rd grade retention on standard diploma acquisition and student outcomes over time: An analysis of Florida's A+ plan.* Retrieved from https://static1
.squarespace.com/static/55e6f66ae4b084d88962a8c7/t/5878c86acd0f6
89b626d535b/1484310635090/Executive+Summary+.pdf

Kohn, A. (2008, Spring). Progressive education: Why it's hard to beat, but also hard to find. *Independent Schools.* Retrieved from https://www.alfiekohn
.org/article/progressive-education/

Krashen, S. (2002a). Defending whole language: The limits of phonics instruction and the efficacy of whole language instruction. *Reading Improvement, 39*(1), 32–42. Retrieved from http://www.sdkrashen.com/content/articles/
2002_defending_whole_language.pdf

Krashen, S. (2002b). Whole language and the great plummet of 1987–92. *Phi Delta Kappan, 83*(10), 748–753.

LaBrant, L. (1931, March). Masquerading. *The English Journal, 20*(3), 244–246.

LaBrant, L. L. (1936). The library and "An experience curriculum in English." *The Elementary English Review, 13*(8), 295–297, 305.

LaBrant, L. (1944, November). The words they know. *The English Journal, 33*(9), 475–480.

LaBrant, L. (1947). Um-brel-la has syllables three. *The Packet, 2*(1), 20–25.

LaBrant, L. (1949). *A genetic approach to language.* Unpublished manuscript. Institute of General Semantics, Lakeville, CT.

Marchitello, M., & Wilhelm, M. (2014, September 26). The cognitive science behind the Common Core. *Center for American Progress.* Retrieved from https://www.americanprogress.org/issues/education-k-12/reports/2014/09/26/97893/the-cognitive-science-behind-the-common-core/

Nathans, A. (1994, December 15). Hooked on Phonics settles with FTC on advertising claims. *Los Angeles Times.* Retrieved from https://www.latimes.com/archives/la-xpm-1994-12-15-mn-9369-story.html

National Council of Teachers of English. (2015). *Resolution on mandatory grade retention and high-stakes testing.* Urbana, IL: Author. Retrieved from http://www2.ncte.org/statement/grade-retention/

National Reading Panel. (2000). *Teaching children to read: Reports of the subgroups.* Washington, DC: U.S. Department of Health and Human Services. Retrieved from https://www.nichd.nih.gov/publications/pubs/nrp/report

Pondiscio, R. (2014, July 3). Why Johnny won't learn to read. *New York Daily News.* Retrieved from https://www.nydailynews.com/opinion/johnny-won-learn-read-article-1.1852715

The Reading First Program's grant application process. (2006, September). Final inspection report. Washington, DC: U.S. Department of Education. Retrieved from https://www2.ed.gov/about/offices/list/oig/aireports/i13f0017.pdf

Robinson, C., & Rogers, T. (2019, October 30). We must raise the bar for evidence in education. *Education Week.* Retrieved form https://www.edweek.org/ew/articles/2019/10/30/we-must-raise-the-bar-for-evidence.html

Rosenblatt, L. (2005). *Making meaning with texts: Selected essays.* Portsmouth, NH: Heinemann.

Sarlin, B., & Thompson, P. (2019, June 9). Unchartered territory: 2020 Democrats back away from charter schools. *NBC News.* Retrieved from https://www.msn.com/en-us/news/politics/unchartered-territory-2020-democrats-back-away-from-charter-schools/ar-AACCeBC

Schwartz, S. (2019a, November 13). In EdReports' first review of early-reading programs, no materials make the grade. *Education Week Teacher.* Retrieved from http://blogs.edweek.org/teachers/teaching_now/2019/11/in_edreports_first_review_of_early-reading_programs_no_materials_make_the_grade.html

Schwartz, S. (2019b, November 12). Schools should follow the 'science of reading,' say national education groups. *Education Week Teacher.* Retrieved from http://blogs.edweek.org/teachers/teaching_now/2019/11/schools_should_follow_the_science_of_reading_say_national_education_groups.html

Sparks, S. D. (2019a, November 8). Screen time up as reading scores drop. Is there a link? *Education Week*. Retrieved from https://www.edweek.org/ew/articles/2019/11/08/screen-time-up-as-reading-scores-drop.html

Sparks, S. D. (2019b, June 6). Want teachers to motivate their students? Teach them how to do it. *Education Week*. Retrieved from https://www.edweek .org/ew/articles/2019/06/06/want-teachers-to-motivate-their-students -teach.html

Spiegel, D. (1998). Silver bullets, babies, and bath water: Literature response groups in a balanced literacy program. *The Reading Teacher, 52*(2), 114–124. Retrieved from www.jstor.org/stable/20202025

Strauss, V. (2018, October 3). Three Time covers show how American attitudes about teachers have changed. *The Washington Post*. Retrieved from https://www.washingtonpost.com/education/2018/10/03/three-time -covers-show-how-american-attitudes-about-teachers-have-changed/

Szalavitz, M. (2017, July 5). Why do we think poor people are poor because of their own bad choices? *The Guardian*. Retrieved from https://www .theguardian.com/us-news/2017/jul/05/us-inequality-poor-people -bad-choices-wealthy-bias

Thomas, P. L., Porfilio, B. J., Gorlewski, J., & Carr, P. R. (Eds.). (2014). *Social context reform: A pedagogy of equity and opportunity*. New York, NY: Routledge.

Trelease, J. (2006). *All in the family: The Bushes and the McGraws*. Retrieved from http://www.trelease-on-reading.com/whatsnu_bush-mcgraw.html

U.S. Department of Education. (2002). *Scientifically based research*. Retrieved from https://www2.ed.gov/nclb/methods/whatworks/research/index .html

Wilde, O. (1891). *The soul of man under socialism*. Retrieved from https://www .marxists.org/reference/archive/wilde-oscar/soul-man/

Will, M. (2017, August 4). Some top U.S. educators went to Finland: Their big takeaway: Empower teachers. *Education Week Teacher*. Retrieved from http://blogs.edweek.org/teachers/teaching_now/2017/08/teachers_ finland.html

Williams, W. C. (1962). The red wheelbarrow. *Poets,org*. Retrieved from https:// poets.org/poem/red-wheelbarrow

WKRC Staff. (2019, November 13). Ohio House passes bill allowing student answers to be scientifically wrong due to religion. *ABC 4 News*. Retrieved from https://abcnews4.com/news/nation-world/ohio-house-passes-bill -allowing-student-answers-to-be-scientifically-wrong-due-to-religion

Wormeli, Rick. (2018, August). Grit and growth mindset: Deficit thinking? *AMLE*. Retrieved from https://www.amle.org/BrowsebyTopic/ WhatsNew/WNDet/TabId/270/ArtMID/888/ArticleID/937/Grit-and -Growth-Mindset-Deficit-Thinking.aspx

Wulf, K. (2019, June 11). What Naomi Wolf and Cokie Roberts teach us about the need for historians. *The Washington Post*. Retrieved from https://

www.washingtonpost.com/outlook/2019/06/11/what-naomi-wolf-cokie
-roberts-teach-us-about-need-historians/

Yatvin, J. (2002). Babes in the woods: The wanderings of the National Reading
Panel. *The Phi Delta Kappan, 83*(5), 364–369.

4

How to End the Reading War and Serve the Literacy Needs of All Students

Shifting Our Deficit Gaze, Asking Different Questions About Literacy

One of the main themes that run through this book is the importance of a historical view of everything, but especially both the realities of how students are educated in the United States (including how students are taught to read) and the patterns of how education debates repeat themselves in the mainstream media and among political leaders. The reading war, I have detailed throughout, has repeated itself in intervals since the earliest decades of the 20th century. In this culminating chapter, I must confess that my work here is also a type of déjà vu since others have made this same effort to expose the "damaging...myths about literacy achievement in the United States" as well as provide solutions to the debate and how students are taught to read (McQuillan, 1998, p. 2).

In fact, McQuillan's (1998) list of myths about literacy from over 20 years ago has mostly been discussed in the previous chapters with an eerie similarity:

How to End the Reading War and Serve the Literacy Needs of All Students, pages 93–122
Copyright © 2020 by Information Age Publishing
All rights of reproduction in any form reserved.

Reading achievement is not in decline, student reading proficiency (however that is defined) is not at a crisis level, there is no explosion of students with dyslexia (in the 1990s, some claimed 1 in 5 students were dyslexic), "students today" are not worse than students in the past, U.S. reading is not far below international students, and WL is not the cause of all these literacy crises.

Before examining, below, ways to end the reading war so that teaching students to read is allowed the spaces necessary to serve the literacy needs of all students, two key concepts need to be understood as foundational for needed big picture changes to occur. First, this discussion has been grounded in critical pedagogy throughout, and all stakeholders in public education as well as how students are taught to read must recognize, as Kincheloe (2005) explains, the following:

> *Every dimension of schooling and every form of educational practice are politically contested spaces* [emphasis added]. Shaped by history and challenged by a wide range of interest groups, educational practice is a fuzzy concept as it takes place in numerous settings, is shaped by a plethora of often-invisible forces, and can operate even in the name of democracy and justice to be totalitarian and oppressive. (p. 2)

Therefore, the reading war debate itself and the actual policies and practices that guide how students are taught to read are always political, a struggle for control over those policies and practices as well as the conditions in which children learn.

Since literacy is fundamental to who any human becomes and what humans believe and do with their lives, teaching and learning reading are incredibly influential parts of any person's life, not to be taken lightly or to be characterized as somehow *not* a political act. For critical educators, then, the reading war and how that impacts student learning is a moral and ethical concern:

> Recognition of these educational politics suggests that teachers take a position and make it understandable to their students. *They do not, however, have the right to impose these positions on their students* [emphasis in original]. . . . To refuse to name the forces that produce human suffering and exploitation is to take a position that supports oppression and powers that perpetuate it. The argument that any position opposing the actions of dominant power wielders is problematic. It is tantamount to saying that one who admits her oppositional political sentiments and makes them known to students is guilty of indoctrination, while one who hides her consent to dominant power and the status quo it has produced from her students is operating in an objective and neutral manner. *Critical pedagogy wants to know who's indoctrinating whom* [emphasis in the original]. (Kincheloe, 2005, p. 11)

In simple terms, all teaching and learning occur in political and ethical spaces; critical educators demand that these realities be named and understood.

But the mainstream media and political debates also occur in political and ethical spaces. Education journalists must be investigated in the same ways as teachers or political leaders—"who's indoctrinating whom." As I discuss in a section below, naïve journalists, for example, are always susceptible to being indoctrinated because they lack historical or scholarly contexts for determining the credibility of the topic they are exploring for the first time (the Columbus Syndrome). Politicians suffer this fate as well, while scholars and educators can be misguided because of their tunnel vision, having looked too narrowly and deeply at the topics journalists and politicians have just discovered. This leads to a second concept that guides this book and final chapter: Good intentions are not enough.

Although writing specifically about the dangers of "good intentions" for educators concerned about equity (economic, racial, etc.) in formal education, Gorski (2008) confronts what I have often identified as "missionary zeal," something that has been identified as a key problem with, for example, Teach for America. While the reading war often includes people with very different views on reading and literacy, the debate is mostly among people who are deeply passionate about reading and education; there is no lack of good intentions or missionary zeal. The "science of reading" reading war, in fact, is characterized by both, especially among those embracing the phrase science of reading and those advocating for identifying students with dyslexia.

So if we combine the two concepts above—education and public debate as inherently political and the limitations of good intentions—we can begin to understand that in order to end the reading war, we are not seeking objectivity, but a reasonably dispassionate informed stance that allows seeking a wide range of evidence and a much more tentative view of science that guides us so that we can implement what students need but also always remain ready and willing to change our understanding and practices as the evidence evolves. But before moving to what must occur in order to end the reading war, I want to offer a section raising a caution, a reader beware, about those who claim that "both sides" in the reading war are equally flawed.

"A Case for Why Both Sides in the 'Reading Wars' Debate Are Wrong—and a Proposed Solution" Is 50% Wrong

In her *The Answer Sheet*, Valerie Strauss (2019) ran a post that represents the problem with both-sides journalism in the context of the reading war: "A case for why both sides in the 'reading wars' debate are wrong—and a proposed solution" by Jeffrey S. Bowers and Peter N. Bowers. Strauss explains before offering the long post:

> This is an unusual post about the "reading wars," that seemingly never-ending battle about how to best teach reading to students—systematic phonics or whole language. This argues that both sides have it wrong, and the authors, two brothers who are literacy experts, suggest a new way. (para. 4)

While the discussion that follows is provocative, often nuanced, and compelling, it makes a mistake common in the false choice between phonics and WL by misdefining WL and then failing to take care when citing research that seems to show neither systematic-intensive phonics nor WL are more effective than the other.

First, let me offer an example of this type of failure in a slightly different context, the powerful and complicated work of Lisa Delpit (2006, 2013). Delpit has made for many years a strong case about the inequity of educational opportunities that cheat Black students (as well as many other vulnerable populations). At times, Delpit's work has been co-opted by conservative voices for educational reform such as advocates for skills approaches to literacy (notably those calling for systematic-intensive phonics and isolated grammar instruction). For clarification, Delpit (2019) makes a very direct refuting of that sort of co-opting:

> I do not advocate a simplistic "basic skills" approach for children outside of the culture of power. It would be (and has been) tragic to operate as if these children were incapable of critical and higher-order thinking and reasoning. Rather, I suggest that schools must provide these children the content that other families from a different cultural orientation provide at home. This does not mean separating children according to family background, but instead, ensuring that each classroom incorporate strategies appropriate for all the children in its confines.

However, the sources of *why* Delpit came to confront how formal education often cheats Black students is an important window into why many continue to misrepresent the reading war by defining *incorrectly* WL (or BL).

As Delpit (2019) explains:

> A doctoral student of my acquaintance was assigned to a writing class to hone his writing skills. The student was placed in the section led by a white professor who utilized a process approach, consisting primarily of having the students write essays and then assemble into groups to edit each other's papers. That procedure infuriated this particular student. He had many angry encounters with the teacher about what she was doing.

> When I told this gentleman that what the teacher was doing was called a process method of teaching writing, his response was, "Well, at least now I know that she thought she was doing something. I thought she was just a fool who couldn't teach and didn't want to try." This sense of being cheated can be so strong that the student may be completely turned off to the educational system.

Yes, this teacher and experience had clearly failed that doctoral student, but if we are careful to note the details of that failure, what we discover is that the teacher had also failed process (or workshop) writing instruction.

Process or workshop writing instruction is far more that peer conferencing; it entails drafting and student choice of topics and text form, conferences with peers *and the instructor, explicit instruction* of all aspects of composing (including grammar, mechanics, and usage) based on the needs of the students revealed in their original essay drafts (typically called mini-lessons), careful and varied reading-like-a-writer experiences with rich texts, and producing final authentic artifacts or writing. To be brief here, Delpit is correct that "other people's children" are disproportionately cheated by reduced curriculum and inadequate instruction, but it is misleading to lay that blame at the feet of misidentified methods—a parallel pattern found in blaming WL or BL for reading failures.

Now, let's circle back to the "both sides are wrong" claim by Jeffrey S. Bowers and Peter N. Bowers. Bowers and Bowers discredit systematic-intensive phonics carefully and fairly, I think. But when they turn to the research on WL, they make no effort to verify if the research cited in fact confirmed that WL was being implemented properly or at all. As I have noted earlier, and as McQuillan (1998) explains in his unpacking of myths from the 1990s, WL was simply never a failure on any small or large scale. As well, Bowers and Bowers make an odd choice about defining what WL is by citing and defining as follows:

> According to foundational theory for whole language, learning to read is just like learning to speak (Goodman, 1967). Given that virtually everyone from every culture learns to speak without any formal instruction in a context of being exposed to meaningful speech, it is concluded that children should learn to read in the same way, naturally, by reading meaningful text. The fact that not all verbal children learn to read with whole language should be a first clue that something is wrong with this theory. (Strauss, 2019)

This dramatically over-simplifies Goodman's work, but also ignores that WL is a philosophy and theory of literacy acquisition (not a fixed set of practices), and then how many have embraced BL.

When we are referring to WL, however, the fundamental problem with discounting WL often rests with not understanding what it is: "Whole language is not a program, package, set of materials, method, practice, or technique; rather, it is a perspective on language and learning that *leads to the acceptance* of certain strategies, methods, materials, and techniques—Dorothy Watson, 1989" (Facts, n.d.). And a failure to acknowledge that "whole language . . . builds on the view that readers and writers integrate all available information in authentic literacy events as they make sense of print. *Whole language teachers don't reject phonics; they put it in its proper place* [emphasis added]" (Goodman, 1993, p. 108).

Let me put this directly: WL does caution against the need for systematic-intensive phonics for *all* children, but the language philosophy endorses entirely that some direct phonics instruction is needed, that each child should receive the amount and type of phonics instruction needed to read independently—not to comply with a reading program, to cover a set of universal standards, or to raise test scores. The argument posed by Bowers and Bowers is correct only if we misdefine WL and fail to critically examine research that claims to be measuring WL effectiveness or if WL was even guiding the instruction. As written, then, the Bowers and Bowers's argument is 50% wrong.

The Education Reform Follies: The Columbus Syndrome

Several years ago, I had a polite argument with a top-level editor at a major newspaper, an editor who routinely was supportive of including my commentaries on the op-ed page. My submission was a strong critique of the accountability era in education, and it specifically detailed that South Carolina was an early and important adopter of the standards/testing-based policies and practices that now mostly define public education across the United States. The argument centered on my outline, noting that South Carolina had accountability legislation in the late 1970s and then standards as well as the Basic Skills Assessment Program (BSAP) and exit exam process being implemented in the early 1980s (when I began teaching as a high school English teacher in 1984).

The editor argued that accountability began way later, in the late 1990s—although I was offering the actual experiences of a classroom teacher who was charged with and held accountable for South Carolina standards and testing from the very first day I entered the classroom in August of 1984. This illustrates, I think, the newest round of education journalism that seems to suggest that the accountability era I have taught under and criticized since the early 1980s is now being declared a failure. One aspect of this so-called shift in political, media, and public attitudes toward education reform based on accountability (standards and high-stakes testing) worth noting is that it reflects my point above about good intentions not being enough.

Many, if not most, education journalists have good intentions; much of the public also has good intentions. Pundits and politicians, I think, often use the veneer of good intentions for political and ideological ends. Nonetheless, this cannot be stressed enough—good intentions are not enough. Yet, acknowledging this is not enough either. Let's consider why good intentions are inadequate.

Education journalists, politicians, and pundits who comment on education are mostly not educators; they have no experience (except as students) or expertise in education. They suffer, I think, from the *Columbus Syndrome*—the mistaken idea that because you witness something (often for the first time as in the case of Christopher Columbus "discovering" the "New World"), you alone have made it come into being and you have *through the simple act of witnessing alone* the right to evaluate and control that which you have witnessed. The editor I argued with in the opening believed education reform had only existed in her time of witnessing it as a journalist, and she resisted listening to me, despite my experiences and expertise in the reality of education reform.

This is the essential flaw with education reform since, as I and many others have been documenting for decades, *education reform is almost entirely driven by those not in education.* Columbus as the embodiment of colonialism—the erasing of people by an aggressive force—is a harsh version of the missionary zeal, I admit, characterizing education reform and education analysis in the media, among politicians, and throughout the public. Missionary zeal can be just as destructive as colonialism, but missionaries believe in their essential goodness, their essential rightness, and that they are ordained to do *to* and not *with* because those to be saved are lesser. But the Columbus Syndrome and missionary zeal are paternalistic and doomed to fail because they depend on ideology instead of experience and expertise. Here, the use of the science of reading in the current reading war is doubly disturbing since it gives weight to what is often mere ideology, the antithesis of science.

Accountability based on standards and high-stakes testing was never the solution in education because that paradigm does not match the essential problems that burden universal public education, problems almost entirely linked to inequity. The same can be said for the silver-bullet claims of the science of reading. And who has been offering credible witnessing to those problems of inequity for well more than a century in the United States? Who has been offering alternatives to education reform for at least the past 20-plus years? Educators and scholars of education—the exact voices demonized, the exact voices ignored.

Now, across the United States, I remain deeply skeptical that we are entering an era when educators and education scholars will, at last, be heard because the current reading war fits a pattern many decades old. My skepticism lies in understanding that genuine and well supported solutions are too complex to be heard, too antithetical to ideologies that remain sacred to the media, the public, and political leadership. Virtually all failures (including education in general and reading) in the United States can be traced to inequity—class privilege and disadvantage, racism, sexism, and so on. Public schools and our students are victims of the greater political refusal to address social inequity, and in-school only reform has been a decades-long effort to distract the public from needed social reform. The science of reading argument is yet another in-school only argument.

Nonetheless, there are very clear messages that have been ignored, and reform that would, over time, drag our education system and even our society toward greater equity. I have made the case, with evidence, dozens and dozens of time. Yet, education reform has resisted and even chosen reform that directly contradicts efforts to create greater equity for children. Here, however, is a list of where to start, a counterargument to education journalists trapped in the Columbus Syndrome, emphasizing the essential understanding that social reform must precede or at least be concurrent to in-school reform while both must seek equity, not accountability:

- food security for all children and their families;
- universal healthcare with a priority on children;
- stable work opportunities that offer robust wages and are divorced from insurance and other so-called "benefits";
- ending the accountability era based on standards and high-stakes testing;
- developing a small-scale assessment system that captures trends but avoids student, teacher, and school labeling and punitive structures;
- ending tracking of students;
- ending grade retention;
- ensuring equitable teacher assignments (experience and certification levels) for all students;

- decreasing the bureaucracy of teacher certification (standards and accreditation) and increasing the academic integrity of education degrees to be comparable with other disciplines;
- supporting teacher and school professional autonomy and implementing mechanisms for transparency, not accountability;
- addressing the inequity of schooling based on race and social class related to funding, class size, technology, facilities, and discipline;
- resisting ranking students, teachers, schools, or states;
- reimagining testing/assessment and grades; and
- adopting a culture of patience, and rejecting the ongoing culture of crisis.

Columbus did not discover the Americas, and the Americas were not a "new world." Even more disturbing is that this mythology allows us to ignore that Columbus did usher in a very long history of horror for native people. On a smaller scale, education reform has echoed that process, teaching an unintended lesson that ideology and missionary zeal are dangerous even when intentions are good.

One key commitment in the United States, then, to end the reading war is to change how the mainstream media drive the national discussion on reading. Journalism must rise above the Columbus Syndrome, depend more carefully on educators and education scholars, and abandon the objective stance of presenting "both sides" of topics regardless of the credibility of those sides. How journalism portrays reading and education is significantly impacted as well by how journalists portray research, how journalists understand (or don't) research, and how both the media and research are shaped by a market economy—as I examine next.

Research, the Media, and the Market: A Cautionary Tale

Reporting in *The New York Times*, Gina Kolata (2019) offers a compelling lede:

> The findings of a large federal study on bypass surgeries and stents call into question the medical care provided to tens of thousands of heart disease patients with blocked coronary arteries, scientists reported at the annual meeting of the American Heart Association on Saturday.
>
> The new study found that patients who received drug therapy alone did not experience more heart attacks or die more often than those who also

received bypass surgery or stents, tiny wire cages used to open narrowed arteries. (para. 1–2)

And Julie Steenhuysen (2019) adds an interesting detail to this major study: "At least two prior studies determined that artery-clearing and stenting or bypass surgery in addition to medical treatment does not significantly lower the risk of heart attacks or death compared with non-invasive medical approaches alone" (para. 4)

But these details may prove to be the most important ones of all:

Over $8 billion worth of coronary stents will be sold annually by 2025, according to a new research report by Global Market Insights, Inc. The increase over the years will be created by an increase in artery diseases coupled with a growing demand for minimally invasive surgeries. (Mraz, 2019, para. 1)

So now let's do the math. If heart doctors shift to what the new research shows, "The nation could save more than $775 million a year by not giving stents to the 31,000 patients who get the devices even though they have no chest pain, Dr. Hochman said," reports Kolata (2019, para. 26). Better and less intrusive patient care, lower overall medical costs for a U.S. healthcare system already overburdened—what is there to keep the medical profession from embracing compelling scientific research? Well, the market of course.

Lower costs come from fewer heart surgeries, meaning heart surgeons lose income—and possibly patients. Keep in mind that while the medical profession decades ago emphasized best practice in prescribing antibiotics (only when bacterial infections are detected), *many doctors found that following best practice led to dissatisfied patients,* who flexed their consumer muscles by finding doctors who would usurp best practice and prescribe the requested antibiotics even when they weren't warranted (Ong et al., 2007). The more recent research on stents and heart disease treatment is a cautionary tale about research, the media, and the market—a cautionary tale that should inform the current call for the science of reading, especially as that impacts children with dyslexia.

That several studies now show the use of stents should be reduced or at least delayed, but that doctors have resisted that evidence calls out for us to ask an important question about scientific research: In whose interest is the research being applied? And in whose interest is that research being reported (or not) and interpreted?

At the International Literacy Association 2019 conference, P. David Pearson, University of California, Berkeley, lays out in about 11 minutes a compelling unpacking of "What Research Really Says About Teaching Reading—and

Why That Still Matters." In this framing talk before a panel discussion, Pearson (2019) confronts the role of media in misinforming the public about research, challenges advocates of "scientific research" who fluctuate between endorsing research and following "common sense," and calls for not ignoring "scientific research" but expanding the types of research relied upon to make teaching and learning decisions (recognizing a broad spectrum of *evidence-based* research that trumps ideology or assumptions).

One of the most compelling examples offered by Pearson (2019) is how the media framed research on reading after the report from the controversial National Reading Panel (NRP), at the center of No Child Left Behind's mandate for scientific research (see Chapter 3). The media headline Pearson highlights is "Systematic, Explicit, Synthetic Phonics Improves Reading Achievement." Yet, the specific study being cited, he explains, actually was far more complicated, and not a simple endorsement of systematic phonics; along with "many other elements . . . , a small but robust effect for a subset of the population is found on a measure that requires kids to *read a list of pseudowords*." This misleading reporting represents the power of not just how media report on research but the inadequacy of journalists interpreting research for the general public (again, in whose interest?).

Pearson (2019) adds that even if we accept the larger NRP report as valid (a thin assumption), the report calls for systematic intensive phonics for Grade 1 students, not older struggling readers. Yet, as Pearson explains, many calling for the science of reading push for systematic phonics programs throughout grades well beyond Grade 1. So there exists several traps in calling for scientific research in education, and more narrowly, in the teaching of reading.

As another example, consider this response from Timothy Shanahan (2019), who lead the NRP, on the effectiveness of dyslexia fonts:

> Over the past decade or so, three new fonts have appeared (Open Dyslexia, Dyslexie, and Read Regular), all claiming—without any empirical evidence—to somehow aid dyslexic readers.
>
> Since then there have been 8 studies into the value of these fonts.
>
> Most of the studies found no improvement in reading rate, accuracy, or eye fixations (Duranovic,et al., 2018; Kuster et al., 2018; Rello & Baeza-Yates, 2013; Wery & Diliberto, 2017). The studies even found that dyslexics—children and adults—preferred reading standard fonts to the special ones (Harley et al., 2016; Kuster et al., 2018; Wery & Diliberto, 2017).
>
> Only one study reported a benefit of any kind—the dyslexic students in this study read faster (Marinus, et al., 2016). This benefit apparently came, not from the font design, but from the spacing within and between words. The

researchers increased the spacings in the standard fonts and the same effect was seen. Masulli (2018) likewise found that larger spacings improved the reading speed of dyslexics—but that effect was apparent with non-dyslexic readers, as well.

Reading faster is a good thing, of course, as long as reading comprehension is maintained. Unfortunately, these studies didn't look at that. (para. 11–15)

The use of dyslexia fonts, then, are driven by the market—consumer demand being met by businesses—but not supported by evidence; neither the claims of the businesses nor the outcomes from implementing the fonts are justified by "scientific evidence." However, the market can be and often is driven by consumers (such as parents of dyslexic children) who are more compelled by marketing than by scientific research.

Just as Hooked on Phonics (see Chapter 3) flourished in two different iterations (the first felled by court rulings that exposed the lack of research backing market claims), *many reading and systematic-intensive phonics programs in education are reinforced by consumer beliefs and marketing but not by scientific research.* Yet the traps around reading programs and "scientific" are extremely complex from two different angles.

First, as noted in several examples above, teaching and learning are likely not served well within a market dynamic whereby parents and students are the consumers with teachers and schools serving the misinformed demands of those consumers. Yes, parents and students have a right to express their need, but they most often lack the expertise to demand *how that need should be met.* Parents of children with reading problems or dyslexia should be demanding that their children be served better and appropriately. But calling for specific policy and practice is outside the purview of those "consumers." (This is the same dynamic in patients seeking doctors who prescribe antibiotics when they are not needed, creating a health hazard for themselves and others when medical best practice is usurped by market demand.)

The second trap, however, is "scientific" itself. As I detailed in Chapter 3, experimental and quasi-experimental research (what we mean by "scientific," as Pearson [2019] discusses) draws causal relationships that can be generalized. By definition, then, generalizable research doesn't address outliers or real-world situations where several factors impact the effectiveness of teaching and learning. The "scientific" trap positions a parent of a child struggling to read, diagnosed with dyslexia, into a problematic corner if that child finds success with dyslexia fonts, a practice not supported by a narrow type of scientific research.

Teaching and teachers must be, instead, guided by evidence, both the evidence of a wide range of research types and the evidence drawn from the individual students in any classroom. To teach is to quilt together what a teacher knows about the field, reading for example, and then what instructional approaches will address where any student is and where any student wishes to go. This, ironically, is the philosophy behind balanced literacy, the approach demonized (usually with false claims and without evidence) by those calling for the science of reading.

The reading war, then, is often fueled by the worst consequences of how the media and the market interpret, ignore, or frame research to parents and students as consumers. Next, I discuss whether or not the media is able to learn from some of these mistakes in the context of education reform, the larger environment in which the reading war thrives.

Education Reform: Warnings Confirmed, But Lessons Learned?

Soon after I began my career as an educator in 1984, I became a serious cyclist. An unexpected hobby sprang from that newfound activity—being my own bicycle mechanic. In fact, over the past 3-plus decades, I have built up dozens of road bicycles from the parts for myself and my friends. In the late 1990s, I bought my first titanium road frameset made by Litespeed.

Not long after I began riding it, I noticed an irritating creaking sound and soon learned that the different metals involved in the various parts often created such problems, notably mounting aluminum bottom bracket cups into the threaded titanium bottom bracket. Several times, I reinstalled that bottom bracket fitting, cleaning, changing greases, and even using thread tape. I worked on the bicycle while mounted on my indoor trainer, and each time, when I tested the bicycle there, the noise was gone. However, once on the open road, the same creaking returned.

Frustrated, I resigned myself to taking the bicycle to a shop mechanic. Like I did, he rebuilt the bottom bracket, multiple times, but each time he went out onto the road to test the bicycle, the creaking noise persisted. After spending an inordinate amount of time fruitlessly working on the bottom bracket, the mechanic called me to report that he eventually discovered the noise was coming from the quick releases on the wheels. In fact, he also shared in exasperation that using aluminum quick releases on titanium dropouts was a common noise problem.

The moral of this story? The mechanic and I were so focused on a solution that we failed to properly evaluate the problem in the beginning, and we both continued to try the same solution over and over even as it failed to work each time. For the professional mechanic, this was particularly disturbing because his obsession with one solution clouded his ability to properly diagnose the situation. For me, there is an added lesson: My process also failed because the bicycle was mounted on my trainer, which clamped the quick releases and created a false environment for testing the problem and the solution.

Overlapping my career as an educator and avocation as a cyclist have been nearly four decades of education reform in the United States. Recently, an interesting phenomenon has occurred, well reflected in this commentary by Van Schoales (2019) in *Education Week*—"Education Reform as We Know It Is Over. What Have We Learned?"—that proclaims:

> The education reform movement as we have known it is over. Top-down federal and state reforms along with big-city reforms have stalled. The political winds for education change have shifted dramatically. Something has ended, and we must learn the lessons of what the movement got right—and wrong. (para. 1)

Contemporary education reform in the United States has followed a pattern characterized by those driving the reform wearing blinders and ear plugs. Around the early 1980s, with the publication of *A Nation at Risk*, the accountability era began, grounded in standards, high-stakes testing, and a laser focus on holding students and their schools accountable.

In the 1980s and 1990s, when I was a public school English teacher, that accountability movement marched forward, driven mostly by state political initiatives that seemed more committed to the next-generation standards and tests than to any sort of goals (which changed constantly also). Despite the disconnect between the promises and outcomes of accountability-based education reform, there were huge political benefits to accountability, best represented by George W. Bush translating the "Texas miracle" (which was thoroughly debunked as no "miracle") during his tenure as governor of Texas into No Child Left Behind (NCLB) as a signature feature of his two-term presidency.

Education reform shifted from a state initiative to a federal one with NCLB—but the outcomes remained quite underwhelming when compared to the promises associated with ever-new standards and tests as well as market-based solutions such as school choice, charter schools, and teacher evaluations linked to testing. The presidency of Barack Obama may have best captured the failure that is education reform committed to accountability since Obama and Secretary of Education Arne Duncan embraced and expanded the policies and beliefs begun under Bush—Common Core as the next-generation standards and concurrent next-generation testing, teacher evaluations linked to those tests and the Brave New World of value-added methods to identify the best teachers and remove the worst, and the rampant expansion of charter schools (although research repeatedly shows that type of schools—private, public, or charter—is not correlated with outcomes).

Throughout these 4 decades, political leaders and the media have pounded the same drum nonetheless—schools are failing in the United States, teachers and administrators practice the "soft bigotry of low expectations," and ratcheting up accountability with better standards and more testing will create schools that are "game changers," proving finally that "zip codes are not destiny" in the U.S. education reform in this accountability era became mostly hollow sloganism—"no excuses" and "zero tolerance" as a couple more examples. Currently, as I examine in this book, we have added the science of reading to our slogans-of-the-day. Yet, all along the way, educational scholars/researchers and classroom teachers firmly and consistently refuted nearly all of the claims of crisis as well as warned political solutions would not bear fruit.

And we were right.

Still, the crisis rhetoric of the Reagan era is no different than the complaints about U.S. public schools today. Four decades of in-school only reform focusing on accountability have accomplished very little except to ensure that children are left behind and to drive away legions of professional educators who can simply no longer labor under false narratives and impossible teaching and learning conditions. The history of public education combined with the current accountability era of schooling in the United States has offered, in fact, some sobering realities about universal public education in the service of democracy.

Those sobering realities are simply so harsh against the myths that many in the U.S. embrace that we refuse to start our education reform by carefully identifying the problems and the causes of those problems—much as the bicycle mechanic and I wasted our time and energy on my bicycle creaking, much as I worked in a false environment to try find a solution. Here's one slogan you won't hear too often: *Public education has not failed its promise to U.S. democracy; we have failed public education.* And here's another slogan you won't hear, maybe at all: *Public schools do not change society; public schools reflect and perpetuate all aspects of the communities and societies they serve.* To focus on the topic of this discussion, we can add: *Reading achievement by students in the*

United States remains more a reflection of poverty, racism, and inequity than a solid measure of reading instruction or student reading ability and desire.

Tax-funded community schools reflect in almost every way the challenges, flaws, and advantages found in the communities they serve. Schools, regardless of the idealistic rhetoric, do not change substantially their communities, or the children who walk their halls. For just one example, my Foundations in Education students tutor in a nearby high-poverty majority-minority middle school. As we debriefed on the last day of class one semester, several students noted that they felt frustrated in the classes they were assigned because those students have had a revolving door of substitute teachers and spend many days without lesson plans or a clear focus on what they are doing. I noted that high-poverty students often experience a great deal of transience and instability in their lives outside of schools, and were then having the same sort of unstable experiences at school. That in-school reality is not a game changer—but a game perpetuator.

In my 36th year as an educator, with over 25 as a scholar/researcher, I am deeply skeptical that anyone with the power to reform education or to reform the education reform movement has in fact learned the lessons I lay out above, or the ones addressed by Schoales (2019). The accountability process in education was destined to fail because the problems with our schools, including our concerns about student reading ability, have little to do with a lack of accountability. But this current era of reform has also done immeasurable harm to students, teachers, and public education as well as reading.

Not only must we finally admit that education problems are a subset of social inequity, but also we must find ways to address that unnecessary harm done during decades of misguided reform—including billions of tax dollars wasted. Those of us ignored during these times had the problems identified all along—gross inequities grounded in systemic poverty, racism, and sexism. The education reform needed, then, is a huge task that involves policies addressing social inequities along with educational inequities, and frankly, I doubt we have the political courage in the United States to acknowledge this or to do anything substantive about it.

Combined with a shift in how the mainstream media cover education and reading, we need a much larger shift in how all stakeholders in public schools envision education reform, moving away from accountability and toward reforms driven by equity. Student reading achievement will improve for almost all students if social inequity is addressed while we also ensure equity in schools such as ensuring greater access to books and high-quality teachers as well as robust learning environments *for all students, especially those students most vulnerable.*

Misreading Cause and Effect in Literacy Instruction: Vocabulary Edition

There are many additional ways to focus on greater equity and better literacy opportunities for all students. For example, a former student of mine in teacher education, who was an English major and is now an early-career teacher, excitedly shared with me that her high school English students have spontaneously begun maintaining a vocabulary list for their course (see Figure 4.1). What is interesting about this vocabulary list? Students are cataloguing the words they are learning simply by hearing this teacher use the language of a highly literate and well-educated person.

I take no credit for this, but this real-world, spontaneous, and rich environment for literacy growth does reflect (although in a more effective way) what I share with my teacher candidates about my 18 years teaching high

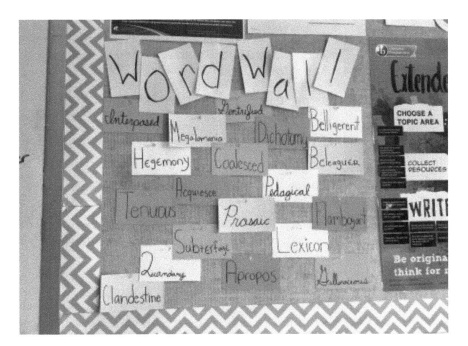

Figure 4.1 Word wall created and maintained by students at Travelers Rest High School (South Carolina).

school English. Eventually, I ended the practice in my English department of issuing grammar textbooks and vocabulary workbooks to all students. Teachers were given sets of both and allowed to use as their professional practice dictated. In my classes, neither were used in any way. As the example above from my former student's class shows, I would model for my students how to discuss literature (texts), films, and popular music, often restating their comments in more sophisticated and complex ways.

Gradually, and spontaneously, my students began to mimic the language and terminology in their discussions and writing. I have experienced a similar pattern in my first-year writing students when students begin to incorporate language and concepts from their main textbooks into our conferences and class discussions. Coincidentally, my former student's excitement over her students' vocabulary activities preceded by a couple days a post on NCTE Connects asking about effective vocabulary instruction. I immediately responded:

> Like grammar instruction, vocabulary instruction is deeply misguided when it is in isolation and vocabulary-for-vocabulary's sake. People are confused and tend to invert erroneously what people with high literacy and large vocabularies demonstrate. Vocabulary is a consequence of rich and extended literacy experiences; cramming vocabulary *into* students is not how you make someone highly literate. In short, if you care about vocabulary, reduce dramatically time and energy spent on vocabulary instruction and focus on rich literacy experiences, notably reading by choice and vibrant discussion. One early-career teacher I know has witnessed her students initiating a vocabulary list of words she teaches them simply through her own expression (her talking to the classes and students); they hear new words almost daily, ask her about them, and are engaged in authentic vocabulary attainment. Also FYI: Power of Common Core to Reshape Vocabulary Instruction Reaches Back to 1944! (Thomas, 2015)

Next, I want to elaborate on some of the key points from this comment to a professional literacy community.

First, the traditional practice of teaching literacy *skills*—grammar, mechanics, usage, and vocabulary, for example—in *isolation and sequentially* to build toward some ideal whole is deeply ingrained but also deeply flawed. I find this to be the result of uncritical assumptions about the power and effectiveness of analysis. Education has embraced a truism that likely isn't true (especially in terms of human literacy): Working from part to whole is easier and better for all learning. How many of us have uttered or been told, kindly, "Let me break this down for you"? Let me pause here and ask you to do a thought experiment (or maybe just focus on a very specific memory).

Have you ever purchased something you had to assemble? Furniture, a swing set, the hellscape that is anything from Little Tikes? These items come with detailed instructions, guiding you from part to whole to construct whatever you have purchased. Have you ever been compelled to dutifully follow those directions, laying out the parts as directed and then meticulously beginning your project? And do you recall that moment when you were mostly lost because you couldn't really decipher the directions? What did you do? Maybe you grabbed the box and began comparing your Frankenstein's monster scattered on the floor with the *whole thing depicted in the picture on the box*?

This urge, some brain research suggests, may be rooted in that only about 1 in 4 people are predisposed to part-to-whole thinking—while 3 in 4 of us work naturally whole-to-part. My argument here about the relationship between part and whole, after almost four decades of teaching and spending much of that studying intently the research on literacy acquisition and growth, is that part and whole are *symbiotic*, working together in ways that defy a linear/sequential model. So I am not arguing for a false dichotomy between part-to-whole and whole-to-part, but arguing for whole-part-whole-part, something not easy to express in words or a diagram.

Here is a powerful example of how traditional assumptions can create ineffective practices. Literacy instruction may not be as efficient or effective as many believe for most of our students in traditional approaches grounded in skills instruction because literacy is wholistic. Next, this flawed set of assumptions is also driven by flipping—and misreading—cause and effect in literacy growth. Yes, highly literate people and sophisticated language are often characterized, for example, by large and complex vocabularies. However, this characteristic is an outcome, an effect.

The mistake too many make in literacy instruction is viewing isolated vocabulary instruction as a cause for rich literacy; thus, extensive vocabulary lists, workbooks, and tests (including nearly fanatical instruction in prefixes, root words, and suffixes) that waste time and energy *better spent* in the real cause of literacy growth—rich literacy experiences such as reading often and deeply by choice and having complex discussions grounded in those rich experiences with a wide variety of texts.

Here is a relatively simple and more accurate truism, then, about reading: A large and nimble vocabulary is an *effect* of rich literacy experiences—not the *cause* of literacy development. Therefore, another way to end the reading war is to transform how we understand literacy and reading, not as a set of discrete skills but as a holistic human behavior. Expression is not simply adding up sounds to create words, and words to create sentences.

Reading and all forms of literacy are highly complex and even haphazard in nature, possibly unique to each person in many ways. For the purposes of this book, then, a healthier and more accurate view of literacy discredits the argument in the science of reading that calls for systematic-intensive phonics instruction for all students.

Negotiating Meaning From Text: "Readers Are Welcome to It if They Wish"

When I finished Jeff VandeMeer's *The Southern Reach Trilogy*, I should add "finally" since I plowed through with glee *Annihilation*, warmed to *Authority* after adjusting to the different style/genre and main character, but sputtered through *Acceptance* out of a sort of self-imposed commitment to read the entire trilogy. On balance, I can fairly say I may have almost no idea what happened in these novels, and I certainly have only some faint urges about what the trilogy means—especially in the sorts of ways we assign meaning in formal schooling such as English courses.

Now approaching 60, having taught for over 34 years, I am afforded something almost no students are allowed: I read entirely by choice, and thus, I can quit any book at any time with no consequences (except my own shame at having not read a book). I still on occasion highlight and annotate the books I read. But no tests, no papers (except I do often blog about the books I read). Traditionally, fictional texts and poetry have been reduced in formal schooling—in English courses—to mere vehicles for "guess what the text means," or more pointedly "guess what the teacher claims the text means." Text meaning in English courses, then, is located often in the authority of the teacher, not in the text itself or the student.

As a high school English teacher, I was always careful to avoid propagandizing students toward "the" singular authoritarian meaning of a text, but I also felt obligated to make students fully aware of the traditional expectations (New Criticism, Advanced Placement testing, etc.) of couching all claims of meaning in the text itself. Students still often struggled with why one meaning held credibility and others did not. One approach to this problem I used was asking students to read William Carlos Williams's (1962) "The Red Wheelbarrow," and then to visualize a wheelbarrow. I went around the room and had the students identify the position of the wheelbarrow in their individual visualizations. I also shared that I always thought of wheelbarrows leaned against a tree because I was warned by my father growing up about not leaving wheelbarrows so that rain water could accumulate and rust out the tub.

From here, we discussed that the poem gives several details—"red," "glazed with rain/water"—but nothing about its physical position. Meaning, then, could work from those *text details*, but students' visualization of the wheelbarrow was a personal response, not an element for claims of academic meaning. I also stressed that students should not think the distinction between academic meaning and personal response suggested that their responses did not matter, or mattered less. However, in formal situations such as testing or assigned critical analysis in courses, most assessments would draw an evaluative judgment (grades), honoring text-based meaning over personal response.

Yet, I remain deeply concerned about how formal schooling, especially narrow versions of literary analysis essays and high-stakes testing, erodes and even poisons students' joy in reading texts by continuing to couch text meaning in the authority of the teacher, which is often a proxy for the authority of the critic (and not the author, or the students as readers). Authors, I often warned my students, did not write their fiction and poetry so teachers could assign them and then have students analyze the text for literary techniques and the ultimate meaning or theme. Many celebrated authors dislike their English courses, and equally reject the literary analysis game.

Author Sara Holbrook (2017), for example, confessed "I can't answer these Texas standardized test questions about my own poems":

> These test questions were just made up, and tragically, incomprehensibly, kids' futures and the evaluations of their teachers will be based on their ability to guess the so-called correct answer to made up questions. (para. 18)

Texas, please know, this was not the author's purpose in writing this poem.

This *tyranny of testing* supplants not only the authority of students as readers, but also the authority of the writer who constructed the text. And Hannah Furness (2018) reports: "Ian McEwan, the award-winning author, has admitted feeling 'a little dubious' about people being compelled to study his books, after helping his son with an essay about his own novel and receiving a C" (para. 1). Furness (2018) adds that McEwan explained:

> "Compelled to read his dad's book—imagine. Poor guy," McEwan added.
>
> "I confess I did give him a tutorial and told him what he should consider. I didn't read his essay but it turned out his teacher disagreed fundamentally with what he said.
>
> "I think he ended up with a C+." (paras. 4–6)

Text meaning determined by the authority of the teacher trumps, again, students constructing meaning and the author as an agent of intent.

And finally, consider Margaret Atwood (2017) discussing her reimagined *The Handmaid's Tale* as a serial TV drama on Hulu:

> When I first began "The Handmaid's Tale" it was called "Offred," the name of its central character. This name is composed of a man's first name, "Fred," and a prefix denoting "belonging to," so it is like "de" in French or "von" in German, or like the suffix "son" in English last names like Williamson. Within this name is concealed another possibility: "offered," denoting a religious offering or a victim offered for sacrifice.
>
> Why do we never learn the real name of the central character, I have often been asked. Because, I reply, so many people throughout history have had their names changed, or have simply disappeared from view. Some have deduced that Offred's real name is June, since, of all the names whispered among the Handmaids in the gymnasium/dormitory, "June" is the only one that never appears again. That was not my original thought but it fits, so readers are welcome to it if they wish. (paras. 9–10)

Having taught *The Handmaid's Tale* for well over a decade in A.P. Literature, and also having written a book on teaching Atwood's writings, I felt my stomach drop when I first read this—forcing myself to recall that I had taught *as authoritative what Atwood refuted*: June as the original given name of Offred. The source of that, for me, was a published critical analysis, in fact.

This caution clarification by Atwood, I believe, speaks to all literacy classes, where text is too often reduced to an assignment, to a game of guess what the teacher wants the student to say this text means. As literacy teachers, of course, we have many responsibilities. Making students aware of traditional and text-based expectations for assigning meaning to text is certainly one of those responsibilities. These examples, then, represent how having a narrow view of reading, and what texts means, like seeing literacy as a set of separate skill, actually works against goals of all students becoming eager, proficient, and critical readers.

But this must not be the only ways in which we invite students to read, enjoy, and then draw meaning from text. Choice in what students read as well as a wide variety of ways for students to respond to text—these must become the expanded set of responsibilities we practice in our classrooms. Occasionally, if not often, we should as teachers be as gracious as Atwood, providing the space for students to read and then respond with their own authority in a class climate grounded in "readers are welcome to it if they wish."

Too often, beneath the details of the reading war is not only a narrow meaning of "scientific" but also a narrow meaning of what it means to read and make meaning from that reading. To expand what counts as reading and meaning can end the reading war while also opening up how we all can make a case for the value in any text. Ending the reading war becomes in part a move to democratize reading and making meaning from text. Ultimately, ending the reading war includes a much larger shift, one that recognizes and then rejects a deficit view of students, learning, and literacy.

From "Remediation" to "No Excuses": The Indignity of Deficit Thinking

Speaking in Savannah, Georgia, March 21, 1861, in his "Corner Stone" Speech, Alexander H. Stephens, vice president of the Confederate States of America, carefully enumerated the justification for secession among Southern states. At length, Stephens addressed slavery: "The new [Confederate] constitution has put at rest, forever, all the agitating questions relating to our peculiar institution African slavery as it exists amongst us the proper status of the negro in our form of civilization" (para. 9). That "proper status"—according to Stephens and the declarations of secession by Georgia, Mississippi, South Carolina, Texas, Virginia—was misrepresented in the U.S. Constitution, that "rested upon the assumption of the equality of races. This was an error" (para. 9).

The Confederacy, instead, embraced "the great truth that the negro is not equal to the white man; that slavery subordination to the superior race is his natural and normal condition" (Stephens, 1861, para. 10). Stephens (1861) chastised the North because "they assume that the negro is equal, and hence conclude that he is entitled to equal privileges and rights with the white man" (para. 10). Stephens called on the triple bedrocks of authority in his statement of the inequality of the races—science, law, and religion:

> This, our new government, is the first, in the history of the world, based upon this great physical, philosophical, and moral truth. This truth has been slow in the process of its development, like all other truths in the various departments of science. (para. 10)

> With us, all of the white race, however high or low, rich or poor, are equal in the eye of the law. Not so with the negro. Subordination is his place. He, by nature, or by the curse against Canaan, is fitted for that condition which he occupies in our system. (para. 12)

While apologists for Southern heritage often remain unable or unwilling to confront the blatant racism of the Confederacy, many today remain nearly universal in our inability or unwillingness to recognize and then confront racism, classism, and sexism in the form of *deficit thinking*. Deficit thinking, as Stephens (1861) represented, is imposing onto groups or individuals deficits (what is lacking compared to what is considered normal) as the primary characteristics of their humanity. In education, deficit thinking is widespread and the foundational tool for formal schooling as an institution that reflects and perpetuates bigotry, inequity, and marginalization of people based on status instead of merit.

Some deficit thinking appears nearly harmless because of its commonplace use—for example, the term and concept "remediation." Remediation as a normal deficit concept is at the heart of the third-grade retention movement masquerading as reading policy, for example. Remediation, however, is built on several flawed assumptions: (a) learning is predictably linear and sequential (see above), (b) so-called skills such as reading can be accurately quantified (as in "grade level"), and (c) some "types" of learning (associated with rates and/or biological ages of the students) are lesser than others (basic skills versus higher-order thinking skills, for example). Remediation also fails a basic point of logic: If remediation is teaching a student something that student doesn't know, isn't all teaching remediation?

One key type of deficit thinking, then, is remediation because in order to remediate educators must first establish "third grade reading" and then test children in order to label them deficient—and thus the ultimate flaw of grade retention is allowing that seemingly scientific (because it is a formula, a calculation) but biased quantifying to represent *all* students. Many key beliefs and practices in the education reform movement, as well, are masks for deficit thinking: the culture of poverty, "grit," the "word gap," and "no excuses." As deficit thinking, all of these are *driven by* and *contribute to* unacknowledged racism and classism (often among those claiming to be fighting bias and inequity).

To say "poverty is not an excuse" for reading achievement or that student success on standardized tests of reading depends on "grit" is to "blame the victim" since the focus of these slogans and the educational practices built on them highlight the students as deficient and thus needing to be "fixed." The lineage from the blunt racism of Stephens to the paternalistic and coded racism/classism of "grit," "no excuses," and the "word gap" is a lineage of deficit thinking. The racism of the Confederacy did not hide behind code, but more than 150 years later, we are faced with finding the will to decode and debunk the deficit thinking that is just as corrosive to individuals and society as corner-stone speeches.

Remediation, grade retention, lessons in "grit," "no excuses" charter schools, strategies to end the "word gap" (see the discussion of isolated vocabulary instruction above)—these all disproportionately target Black, Brown, and poor children and creates a distracting category under which they all are labeled, failed readers. Those beliefs and practices, however, do not validate claims of deficient children, but expose a deficit of basic humanity among those in positions to honor the dignity of all children, but instead continue to choose otherwise.

About 100 years after Stephens's racist declaration of secession, author Ralph Ellison (1963) concluded a different perspective in "What These Children Are Like": "I'm fascinated by this whole question of language . . ." (para. 23). Ellison explained, "The great body of Negro slang—that unorthodox language—exists," adding,

> precisely because Negroes need words which will communicate, which will designate the objects, processes, manners and subtleties of their urban experience with the least amount of distortion from the outside. So the problem is, once again, what do we choose and what do we reject of that which the greater society makes available? These kids with whom we're concerned, these dropouts, are living critics of their environment, of our society and our educational system, and they are quite savage critics of some of their teachers. (para. 24)

Ellison's (1963) lecture to teachers was an extended rejection of deficit thinking, a powerful refusal to see Black children and anyone's language as deficient. His talk ended with a stirring plea relevant during the "science of reading" reading war:

> I don't know what intelligence is. But this I do know, both from life and from literature: whenever you reduce human life to two plus two equals four, the human element within the human animal says, "I don't give a damn." You can work on that basis, but the kids cannot. If you can show me how I can cling to that which is real to me, while teaching me a way into the larger society, then I will not only drop my defenses and my hostility, but I will sing your praises and help you to make the desert bear fruit. (para. 25)

Deficit thinking in its many forms is fruitless for its indignity.

To end the reading war, a comprehensive shift must occur like Ellison's, viewing language, literacy, reading, teaching, learning, and students not in ways that measure them against a fixed set of characteristics, but focusing on the strengths and what potential lies in a diverse set of circumstances and possible outcomes. Humans and our coming to read are equally unique and unpredictable; thus, we should be asking different questions than why aren't teachers using the science of reading.

Shifting Our Deficit Gaze, Asking Different Questions About Literacy

"Poor Kids and the 'Word Gap'" opens with an important admission by Jessica Lahey (2014): The Horace Mann ideal that education is the "great equalizer" has not materialized (or at least, has eroded). While the impact of education appears powerful *within* class and race categories, educational attainment remains ineffective in overcoming social inequity among social classes and races.

As the article title states, however, Lahey (2014) turns to the *word gap*—a popular and repeated entry point for discussing the educational differences among social classes and races of children. Quoting a Clinton Foundation report, Lahey equates that "word gap" with childhood hunger and food insecurity before detailing the Obama administration's initiative to bridge that socioeconomic word gap. Lahey's article, the Clinton Foundation, and the Obama initiative are all sincerely grounded in good intentions (see above), and all rightfully highlight the need to address the inequity of education in the United States that mirrors the social inequities a rising and high percentage of impoverished children experience.

But, once again, the problem persists that we remain committed to a deficit gaze, one that ultimately blames the parents of children in poverty (often the mother) for the word gap. Looking closely at the Clinton Foundation report (Clinton Foundation, n.d.), in fact, reveals that Hart and Risley's 1995 research (e.g., the chart on page 10 of the Clinton Foundation report) continues to anchor assumptions that the quantity and quality of words are linked to both the socioeconomic status of a child's home and then the child's ability to succeed once in formal schooling. As Dudley-Marling and Lucas (2009) emphasize, the foundational word gap study by Hart and Risley and pathologizing the language of impoverished students are misguided and misleading because of the essential deficit perspectives embedded in each, perspectives reflecting and perpetuating stereotypes. *Pathologizing* language means that the language itself is seen as a "sickness" and thus what must be "treated"—including the concurrent implication that the host of the language, the child, is also diseased and must be cured.

As well, research in the United Kingdom reveals that the dynamic among literacy, social class, and educational attainment is complex, but also powerful. Pleasure reading and even the quality of that reading appear to increase literacy in adults, Sullivan and Brown detail. Sullivan (2014) reaches two important conclusions: the need to protect the library and the importance of books in the child's home. This focus—on strategies for enriching the literacy of children born into impoverished homes and communities—offers important ways for shifting our deficit gaze away from blaming the victims of poverty and toward systemic causes for characteristics (e.g., word gap) so that we can develop policy to prevent the conditions in the first place and also create contexts for alleviating inequity that already exists.

The great challenges facing the United States and our disturbingly high percentage of children living in poverty are social inequities linked to classism and racism. We must admit these problems, and then we must address them directly (and not by clinging to idealistic beliefs such as education will be the "great equalizer"). But we must also address directly the existing inequities reflected in the homes and education of impoverished children. Let's not blame high-poverty mothers; instead, let's develop policies that provide books for children in their homes while we commit to social programs that allow impoverished families the sort of security and opportunities supporting them in their roles as a child's first teachers. Let's not diagnose and then treat impoverished children and their literacy *as the science of reading argument does by overemphasizing dyslexia and systematic-intensive phonics*; instead, let's ensure that all children have rich, diverse, and engaging formal schooling experiences.

The deficit gaze fails because it focuses on individuals and not the conditions within which people find themselves (through no fault of their own). Regardless of good intentions, we must shift our deficit gaze and begin to ask different questions so we can create new and more humane answers. Questions being raised about the science of reading, teacher reading practices, and teacher education are merely distractions in the same ways as all versions of the reading war over the past century.

So this book is intended to focus on a much larger question: How do we end the reading war as distraction in order to serve the literacy needs of all students? As I have detailed in this chapter, the answer is complex and rests mostly at the level of changing fundamental beliefs about language, literacy acquisition, children, teaching, and learning. In short, reading and literacy are far too complex to be reduced to a narrow definition of "science," but acquiring literacy and the ability to read independently, eagerly, and critically can be well supported by our formal schooling if we are far more patient and far more positive about both language and reading.

WL and BL have always offered an all-inclusive framework for supporting teachers making the sorts of professional and complex decisions necessary to attend to any and every child—those with huge advantages and reading with what appears to be ease as well as those who struggle and seem to have reading "problems" that may be a special need or simply may need more time and strategies not identified by so-called high-quality scientific studies.

The science of reading movement demands "all student must" and rationalizes practices that will over-identify children as having special needs (dyslexia) when they are simply developing at rates outside predetermined formulas that dehumanize children and their teachers. The science of reading is lending far too much power to reading programs—systematic-intensive phonics for *all* students—that will certainly force teachers and students to fulfill the program even when that process is not in the best interest of some students. The science of reading will allow many false positives about students being proficient in reading because "reading" is reduced to decoding at the expense of critical literacy and eagerness to read.

Despite the good intentions of many journalists and politicians, not all is settled about how best to teach reading just as not all is settled about what we know and understand about being fully human, which includes being literate, able, and eager to read. Yet, we know a great deal about how to foster critical and eager readers, and have known the power of poverty and inequity to stifle literacy for many decades. We have also known about the power of access to books in children's home and schools, especially when that access is combined with supporting any child's choices about what to read and how to respond to those texts.

The current science of reading version of the reading war is not about reading, however. It is about beliefs and an unhealthy urge to control children, teachers, and literacy. Ending the reading war is about releasing those urges of control that lie beneath claims that science is settled. Nothing is easy about this, but it is remarkably simple: Every child deserves whatever that child needs to be an eager and critical literate human; however, there simply is not a single prescription for what that need may be for any child.

Taking sides in the reading war becomes a march to winning a battle, missing the goals of why the war exists in the first place; this is the essential failure of all reading programs that focus on the program and not the students, not the goals of literacy. We can do better, and we must do better.

References

Atwood, M. (2017, March 10). Margaret Atwood on what 'The Handmaid's Tale' means in the age of Trump. *The New York Times*. Retrieved from https://www

.nytimes.com/2017/03/10/books/review/margaret-atwood-handmaids
-tale-age-of-trump.html

Clinton Foundation. (n.d.). *Preparing America's children for success in the 21st century: Too small to fail.* Retrieved from http://www.clintonfoundation.org/files/2s2f_framingreport_v2r3.pdf

Delpit, L. (2019). Lisa Delpit on power and pedagogy. *Works & Days.* Retrieved from https://newlearningonline.com/new-learning/chapter-8/lisa-delpit-on-power-and-pedagogy

Delpit, L. (2013). *"Multiplication is for white people": Raising expectations for other people's children.* New York, NY: The New Press.

Delpit, L. (2006). *Other people's children: Cultural conflict in the classroom.* New York, NY: The New Press.

Dudley-Marling, C., & Lucas, K. (2009, May). Pathologizing the language and culture of poor children. *Language Arts, 86*(5), 362–370.

Ellison, R. (1963, September). What these children are like. *Teaching American History.* Retrieved from https://teachingamericanhistory.org/library/document/what-these-children-are-like/

Facts: On the nature of whole language education. (n.d.). Heinemann. Retrieved from https://www.heinemann.com/shared/onlineresources/08894/08894f6.html

Furness, H. (2018, May 8). Ian McEwan 'dubious' about schools studying his books, after he helped son with essay and got a C+. *The Telegraph.* Retrieved from https://www.telegraph.co.uk/news/2018/05/06/ian-mcewan-dubious-schools-studying-books-helped-son-essay-got/

Goodman, K. (1993). *Phonics phacts.* Portsmouth, NH: Heinemann.

Gorski, P. C. (2008). Good intentions are not enough: A decolonizing intercultural education. *Intercultural Education, 19*(6), 515–525.

Hart, B., & Risley, T. R. (2003, Spring). The early catastrophe: The 30 million word gap by age 3. *American Educator.* Retrieved from https://www.aft.org/sites/default/files/periodicals/TheEarlyCatastrophe.pdf

Holbrook, S. (2017, January 5). I can't answer these Texas standardized test questions about my own poems. *Huffington Post.* Retrieved from https://www.huffpost.com/entry/standardized-tests-are-so-bad-i-cant-answer-these_b_586d5517e4b0c3539e80c341

Kincheloe, J. L. (2005). *Critical pedagogy primer. 2nd ed.* New York, NY: Peter Lang USA.

Kolata, G. (2019, November 16). Surgery for blocked arteries is often unwarranted, researchers find. *The New York Times.* Retrieved from https://www.nytimes.com/2019/11/16/health/heart-disease-stents-bypass.html

Lahey, J. (2014. October 16). Poor kids and the "word gap." *The Atlantic.* Retrieved from https://www.theatlantic.com/education/archive/2014/10/american-kids-are-starving-for-words/381552/

McQuillan, J. (1998). *The literary crisis: False claims, real solutions.* Portsmouth, NH: Heinemann.

Mraz, S. (2019, November 6). Coronary stent market to hit $8 billion by 2025. *Machine Design.* Retrieved from https://www.machinedesign.com/mechanical-motion-systems/article/21838287/coronary-stent-market-to-hit-8-billion-by-2025

Ong, S., Nakase, J., Moran, G. J., Karras, D. J., Kuehnert, M. J., & Talan, D. A. (2007). Antibiotic use for emergency department patients with upper respiratory infections: Prescribing practices, patient expectations, and patient satisfaction. *Annals of Emergency Medicine, 50*(3), 213–220.

Pearson, P. D. (2019, October 12). *What research really says about teaching reading–and why that still matters* [Video]. International Literacy Association 2019 Conference. Retrieved from https://ila.digitellinc.com/ila/sessions/123/view

Schoales, V. (2019, April 25). Education reform as we know it is over. What have we learned? *Education Week.* Retrieved from https://www.edweek.org/ew/articles/2019/04/26/education-reform-as-we-know-it-is.html

Shanahan, T. (2019, November 16). What about special fonts for kids with dyslexia or other reading problems? *Shanahan on Literacy.* Retrieved from https://www.shanahanonliteracy.com/blog/what-about-special-fonts-for-kids-with-dyslexia-or-other-reading-problems

Steenhuysen, J. (2019, November 16). Stents no better than drugs for many heart patients: U.S. study. *KFGO.* Retrieved from https://kfgo.com/news/articles/2019/nov/16/stents-no-better-than-drugs-for-many-heart-patients-us-study/958129/?refer-section=health

Stephens, A. H. (1861, March 21). *"Corner stone" speech: Teaching American History.* Retrieved from http://web.archive.org/web/20130822142313/http://teachingamericanhistory.org/library/document/cornerstone-speech/

Strauss, V. (2019, March 27). A case for why both sides in the 'reading wars' debate are wrong—and a proposed solution. *The Washington Post.* Retrieved from https://www.washingtonpost.com/education/2019/03/27/case-why-both-sides-reading-wars-debate-are-wrong-proposed-solution/

Sullivan, A. (2014, November 6). Your vocabulary aged 40 depends on how much you read as a teenager. *The Conversation.* Retrieved from https://theconversation.com/your-vocabulary-aged-40-depends-on-how-much-you-read-as-a-teenager-33852

Thomas, P. L. (2015, May 17). Power of Common Core to reshape vocabulary instruction reaches back to 1944! *Radical Eyes for Equity.* Retrieved from https://radicalscholarship.wordpress.com/2015/05/17/power-of-common-core-to-reshape-vocabulary-instruction-reaches-back-to-1944/

CONCLUSION

The Science of Literacy

A 36-Year Journey and Counting

Science is not a hammer.[1]

Science is an old-growth forest, each tree an organic thing. Think of a tree as a theory. At any moment that tree (theory) is fully a tree but not *the tree it will become.* As a tree grows, it becomes more robust, a stronger trunk, deeper roots. If we inspect that trunk, we find rings detailing the history of how that tree became stronger with age. Theories too are not simply the result of fixed (or settled) evidence, but an accumulation of evidence, an accumulation that evolves over time.

Science, like that old-growth forest, is never settled, never finished, but it is always at any moment the best that it can be in terms of being a forest and in terms of the trees being the trees of that moment. You see, *science is also organic,* not yet the forest or trees it can and will become. Old-growth forests are also characterized by being untouched by humans, and while science is the product of humans, science often seeks ways to limit the flaws of that human contact (a lofty and unattainable goal, but one that helps science aspire toward truth and Truth).

How to End the Reading War and Serve the Literacy Needs of All Students, pages 123–127
Copyright © 2020 by Information Age Publishing
123

Science ultimately is aspirational; it can never be settled, fixed, or finished, and anyone using science as a hammer is, in fact, not being scientific.

Science is not a hammer.

Science is an old-growth forest, each tree an organic thing.

•   •   •

Viewing science as a hammer is the fatal flaw of the "science of reading" version of the reading war that has gained momentum in 2019. Advocates of the science of reading begin by claiming that this science is settled:

> In spite of the current discussions, the science on this instructional issue is settled. Castles, Rastle, & Nation (2018) lay out that there is a clear progression to effective literacy instruction. First and foremost, children need to understand the principles of spelling-sound correspondences and to solidify a store of high-frequency words to read words and phrases fluently. Most children need explicit teaching to build this knowledge. After decoding and high-frequency words are established, more attention can be devoted to comprehension with a focus on making meaning. Castles et al. (2018) offer a logical and research-based model. In spite of this research, educators remain without consensus about what is most important—phonics instruction or a focus on comprehension. (Stukey & Fugnitto, 2019, para. 2)

Science is not a hammer, neither is it to be used to bludgeon nor is it a singular tool. In fact, especially for education as well as teaching literacy, science is a much broader spectrum of evidence than science of reading advocates are arguing, committed as they are in the neurosciences. The science needed to guide real-world teaching of literacy is an old-growth forest of many types of trees at different stages of growth. For example, I primarily have been a teacher of writing for 36 years and counting. I have taught students from ninth grade through graduate courses.

As a scholar of teaching writing, I am well versed in the experimental/quasi-experimental research base on teaching writing as well as a huge and complex body of qualitative research. I also have 36 years of experience with thousands of students. All of that is at my disposal as I teach any student to write, an act that for me is highly individualized—even when I taught 100–125 high school students 5 days a week.

The generalizations and controls that result from and govern experimental/quasi-experimental research (which is dominant in neuroscience) are informative (but not prescriptive) for me as a teacher since my work tends to be with many different outliers—humans, that is—who may thrive with practices outside the constraints of narrow types of science.

I don't use science as a hammer because students are fragile things, and instruction that treats them all as 10-penny nails is unwarranted.

•   •   •

You may be thinking about climate change, evolutionary science, or vaccinations—all of which many people would argue are settled science. "Settled," I think, remains a problematic word even in those contexts. All science based in experimental/quasi-experimental research when properly vetted (reviewed by experts in the field) is compelling, compelling to the point that it feels settled, compelling to the point that *we must act in ways that confirm it is settled* even as we are aware this tree may grow.

Since all science remains in the replication loop, we are best off calling even the largest tree with the most powerful trunk and deepest roots "compelling," not settled.

In qualitative research (no generalizations or claims of cause/effect), "compelling" is the best we can hope for, but much of that research remains compelling in day-to-day realities of teaching, although with caveats about the evidence not reaching standards of generalizability and the conditions of the evidence not bound by controls.

•   •   •

Let me end with an anecdote, what some would call *not* scientific. It is the story of having taught writing for 36 years and counting, and still being very cautious about my practice and very nervous about the fate of my field of teaching writing. Actually this is an anecdote about gathering anecdotal evidence, the sort of scientific teaching that John Dewey envisioned for progressive educators.

I always spend the last class of my first-year writing seminars by discussing with students what has worked and what I should do differently in the future. I also use this class to re-emphasize that my overarching goals for these classes are about fostering in them greater authority and autonomy as students and writers about to run the gauntlet of three-and-a-half additional years (or more) of college.

One recent fall, students argued for having Essay 1 turned in earlier, allowing more time and class sessions for Essay 3 (the academically cited essay), and moving Essay 4 earlier to leave more time for the revised submission. We fleshed out these requests against the goals of the course, and ultimately, I found their anecdotal feedback compelling. My schedule for the next fall was revised.

As the professor, as well, I have reflected on how to better encourage students to revise their essays and not simply address what I have marked for them. I discussed this problem with another teacher, and am considering a new policy on how students should resubmit their essays. In the past, I have required students to resubmit essays in clean Word files—track changes, comments, and highlighting all removed. Part of that requirement was aimed at helping students better use Word as a tool, but I also have trouble reviewing Word files that are busy.

However, as I discussed student revision with a friend who teaches writing, I thought about how students having the track changes visible for *their revisions* would show them how much, or how little, they actually revised. Visible track changes can be a very effective teaching tool. So my new policy may be that students submit two Word files, one clean and one with only the track changes of their revisions (with the file including "TC").

This, then, is a brief anecdote about how I teach scientifically as a professional educator, a writer, and an expert in literacy. I teach with caution, I resist teaching with a hammer. This means that when some students demonstrate a need for a type of instruction not supported by a narrow type of research, I still provide the student with that instruction. We may even experiment with a range of strategies until the student feels capable on their own.

I am always cautious, but I am also nervous because while the science of reading movement is in full stride, I see on the horizon a similar fate for the teaching of writing: "Scientific evidence on how to teach writing is slim," some claim (Barshay, 2019).

I suspect the mainstream media will discover a field that already exists, has for a century or more. I suspect the allure of "science" will blind that media and those who also feel passionate about the dismal state of student writing.

So somewhat preemptively, I want to offer about the teaching of writing:

Science is not a hammer.

Science is an old-growth forest, each tree an organic thing.

Note

1. See the law of the instrument, also known as the law of the hammer.

References

Barshay, J. (2019, November 4). Scientific evidence on how to teach writing is slim. *The Hechinger Report.* Retrieved from https://hechingerreport.org/scientific-evidence-on-how-to-teach-writing-is-slim/

Stukey, M. R., & Fugnitto, G. (2019, August 26). The settled science of teaching reading—part I. *Collaborative Circle Blog.* Retrieved from https://www.collaborativeclassroom.org/blog/the-settled-science-of-teaching-reading-part-1/

Recommended Reading

Stephen Krashen (access free online at http://www.sdkrashen.com/)

Lou LaBrant (access selected works at https://loulabrant.wordpress.com/)

Books

- *Literacy Crises: False Claims and Real Solutions*, Jeff McQuillan
- *The Manufactured Crisis*, David C. Berliner and Bruce J. Biddle
- *Collateral Damage: How High-Stakes Testing Corrupts America's Schools*, Sharon L. Nichols and David C. Berliner
- *Readicide: How Schools Are Killing Reading and What You Can Do About It*, Kelly Gallagher
- *Reading Against Democracy: The Broken Promises of Reading Instruction*, Patrick Shannon
- *Beginning to Read and the Spin Doctors of Science, In Defense of Our Children: When Politics, Profit and Education Collide, Resisting Reading Mandates: How to Triumph with the Truth*, Denny Taylor

- *Good to Great Teaching: Focusing on the Literacy Work That Matters*, Mary Howard
- *Big Brother and the National Reading Curriculum: How Ideology Trumps Evidence*; *What Really Matters for Struggling Readers: Designing Research-Based Programs (3rd Edition)*, Richard Allington
- *The Book Whisperer: Awakening the Inner Reader in Every Child*, Donalyn Miller
- *21st Century Literacy: If We Are Scripted, Are We Literate?*, Renita Schmidt and P.L. Thomas
- *Reading for Profit: How the Bottom Line Leaves Kids Behind?*, Bess Altwerger
- *Reading the Naked Truth: Literacy, Legislation and Lies*; *Reading Lessons: The Debate over Literacy*; *Misreading Reading: The Bad Science That Hurts Children*, Gerald Cole
- *One Size Fits Few: The Folly of Educational Standards*, Susan Ohanian
- *Lou LaBrant—A Woman's Life, a Teacher's Life*, Paul Thomas
- *Parental Choice?: A Critical Reconsideration of Choice and the Debate About Choice*, P. L. Thomas
- *The Struggle for the American Curriculum, 1893–1958*, 3rd ed., Herb Kliebard
- *Reading Educational Research: How to Avoid Getting Statistically Snookered*, Gerald Bracey
- *Education and the Cult of Efficiency: A Study of the Social Forces That Have Shaped the Administration of the Public Schools*, Raymond E. Callahan
- *Making Meaning With Texts: Selected Essays*, Louise Rosenblatt
- *"Multiplication Is for White People": Raising Expectations for Other People's Children*; *Other People's Children: Cultural Conflict in the Classroom*, Lisa Delpit
- *Phonics Phacts*; *The Truth About DIBELS: What It Is—What It Does*; *On Reading*, Kenneth Goodman

APPENDIX **B**

Checklist

Media Coverage of the "Science of Reading"

Several years ago while preparing the first edition (2013) of *De-testing and De-grading Schools: Authentic Alternatives to Accountability and Standardization*, I came to know Peter DeWitt as a highly praised principal who wrote in that volume about no-testing week at his school. His work and career have shifted since then, but I have remained in contact through his public writing. Coinciding with a mostly fruitless Twitter debate about how the media continues to misrepresent the challenges and realities of teaching reading, then, I was strongly drawn to DeWitt's (2019) "3 Reasons I Do Not Engage in Twitter Debates."

Much of his examination of the paradox that is social media is extremely compelling to me; his three reasons, in fact, resonate powerfully: Social media debates are rarely about common understanding, they make you look really crazy to onlookers, and he's not good at them. When I find myself crossing (foolishly) DeWitt's pointed line into social media debate, I try to justify the effort by this (mostly idealistic and probably misguided) justification: Making a nuanced and detailed case, even with the limitations

How to End the Reading War and Serve the Literacy Needs of All Students, pages 131–136
131

of Twitter and other platforms, will likely not persuade the Twitter thread participants, but can provide a context for learning to those observing the discussion.

However, I find DeWitt's conclusions hold fast, and thus, offering here the details and the nuance has a better, although also limited, potential for changing the reading war dialogue and reaching more understanding. Instead of providing yet another discrediting of yet another media misrepresentation of the "science of reading," I offer here a checklist for those who want to navigate the media coverage of the reading war in an informed and critical way.

Mainstream media education journalism is routinely bad because of some broad problems inherent in journalism: Journalists tend to be generalists, and media assume a journalist can and should cover specialized fields; journalism remains bound to a "both sides" coverage of topics that misrepresents the actual balance of evidence in those specialized fields; and as I outline below, mainstream media tend to be trapped in a sort of *presentism* that lacks historical context (all of which has been examined more carefully in the preceding chapters).

Below, with additional sources (easily search on the Internet or in the references of this volume) to support and illuminate the problems, is a checklist for critically analyzing mainstream media's coverage of the science of reading:

☐ *Misrepresenting balanced literacy (BL), whole language (WL) to discredit them.* To evaluate media coverage of reading instruction, know that reading ideologies such as BL and WL suffer very complex realities. As explained in Chapter 3, even when teachers or schools claim to be implementing BL or WL, there is ample evidence that traditional and more isolated practices are actually in place. Second, and extremely important to the current and historical versions of the reading wars, both BL and WL recognize and endorse a significant place for phonics instruction in early literacy; as Stephen Krashen (2017) explains pointedly: "Zero Phonics. This view claims that direct teaching is not necessary or even helpful. I am unaware of any professional who holds this position" (para. 6).

Resources
- "Defending Whole Language: The Limits of Phonics Instruction and the Efficacy of Whole Language Instruction," Stephen Krashen
- "Whole Language and the Great Plummet of 1987–92," Stephen Krashen

- *Literacy at the Crossroads: Crucial Talk About Reading, Writing, and Other Teaching Dilemmas*, Regie Routman
- Facts: On the nature of whole language education (Heinemann)
- "Silver Bullets, Babies, and Bath Water: Literature Response Groups in a Balanced Literacy Program," Dixie Lee Spiegel

☐ *Misrepresenting the complex role of phonics in reading in order to advocate for phonics programs.* Related to the first point above, phonics advocacy tends to suggest falsely that some literacy experts support no phonics instruction and that all children must receive systematic-intensive phonics instruction; these extreme polarities distort, ironically, what the broad and complex research base does show about how children learn to read as well as the role of phonics in that process.

Resources
- "To Read or Not to Read: Decoding Synthetic Phonics," Andrew Davis
- "Literacy: Phonemic Awareness and Phonics," Stephen Krashen
- *The Literacy Crisis False Claims Real Solutions*, Jeff McQuillan

☐ *Lacking historical context about the recurring "reading wars" and the false narratives of failing to teach children to read.* The media, the public, and political leaders have chosen a crisis narrative for teaching reading throughout the 20th and into the 21st century. That framing as crisis has mostly obscured both the problems that do limit effective reading instruction and the complex nature of teaching reading as well as the current research base on teaching and literacy development.

Resource
- "What Shall We Do About Reading Today?: A Symposium Research in Language" (1947), Lou LaBrant

☐ *Overemphasizing/misrepresenting National Reading Panel (NRP) value and ignoring it as a narrow and politically skewed report.* A central component of No Child Left Behind was the NRP; however, as a key member of the panel has detailed, that report was neither a comprehensive and valid overview of the then-current state of research on teaching reading nor a foundational tool for guiding reading practices or policy. Yet, media coverage routinely references the NRP as gold-standard research and laments its lack of impact (although the NRP report did spawn a disturbing scandal concerning federal funding and textbook adoptions).

Resources
- ▪ "Babes in the Woods: The Wanderings of the National Reading Panel," Joanne Yatvin
- ▪ "Did Reading First Work?," Stephen Krashen
- ▪ "My Experiences in Teaching Reading and Being a Member of the National Reading Panel," Joanne Yatvin
- ▪ "I Told You So! The Misinterpretation and Misuse of The National Reading Panel Report," Joanne Yatvin
- ▪ "Beyond Smoke and Mirrors: A Critique of the National Reading Panel Report on Phonics," Elaine M. Garan

☐ *Citing bogus reports from discredited think tanks such as the National Council of Teacher Quality (NCTQ).* Well over a decade ago, Gerald Bracey (2006) warned about the growing influence of agenda-driven think tanks aggressively promoting reports before they are peer-reviewed; since the mainstream media and most journalists are underfunded and overworked, press-release journalism has become more and more common, especially regarding education and often in terms of how so-called research is framed for the public. With the recent focus on the science of reading, the scapegoat of the day is teacher education; the narrative goes that teachers today do not know the science of reading because teacher education programs do not teach the science of reading. Often as proof, the mainstream media resort to anecdote (they talk to a teacher or two who claims not to have been taught the science of reading) and cite bogus reports masquerading as research—notably the work of NCTQ, a think-tank that has aggressively and falsely attacked teacher education in report after report using slip-shod methods and devious processes to gather the data claim to analyze.

Resources
- ▪ NEPC Review: 2018 Teacher Prep Review (National Council on Teacher Quality, April 2018)
- ▪ "Review of Learning About Learning: What Every New Teacher Needs to Know," P. L. Thomas and Christian Z. Goering

☐ *Scapegoating teacher education while ignoring two greatest influences on reading: Poverty and reading programs adopted to comply with standards and high-stakes testing.* There is ample room to criticize teacher education, particularly focusing on the problems with credentialing and the flaws inherent in the accreditation process, but the current media urge to blame teacher education for either how reading is taught or the errors in how reading is taught distracts from some hard facts about measurable reading achievement:

First, standardized testing of all kinds are more strongly correlated with socioeconomic and out-of-school factors than either teacher, teaching, or school quality; and this blame-teacher-education narrative glosses over that almost all reading instruction in U.S. public schools is mandated by standards, high-stakes testing, and adopted reading programs regardless of what teachers learned in their certification program.

Resources
- "Teachers Matter, But So Do Words," Matthew Di Carlo
- "Masquerading" (1931), Lou LaBrant

☐ *Conflating needs of students with special needs and needs of the general population of students.* The genesis of the most recent version of the reading war that focuses on the science of reading is grounded in a growing advocacy for children either not diagnosed or misdiagnosed for issues related to dyslexia. Parents of those children have been very politically active, and while their concerns for children with special needs are valid, the media and politicians have overreacted to that narrow issue and overgeneralized the needs of those students to all students. This advocacy has also run roughshod over the actual and more nuanced research base on dyslexia itself. In short, parents advocating for their children should be honored and heard, but parents should not be driving reading instruction or reading policy.

Resource
- 2016 International Literacy Associations Reading Advisory on Dyslexia

☐ *Emphasizing voices of cognitive scientists over literacy professionals.* Two common patterns in media coverage of education and specifically reading are that journalists perpetuate both a gender and a discipline bias in whose voices are highlighted; notably, mostly men who are cognitive scientists are used to drive the agenda while women who are literacy practitioners and scholars are either ignored, marginalized as "critics," or scapegoated as misguided advocates of BL or WL.

☐ *Trusting silver-bullet, one-size-fits-all claims about teaching and learning.* Fundamentally, the historical and current flaw in the reading war, even one framed as the science of reading, is that phonics advocacy reaches for "all students must have systematic-intensive phonics programs," buoyed recently by "but intensive phonics programs won't hurt any students." However, teaching and learning prove to be far more complex than these claims. If we return to BL as a reading philosophy, we can emphasize that each child (not all children) should receive the type and amount of direct phonics instruction they need to begin and then grow as readers; that type and amount is difficult to prescribe, and often children are mis-served when systematic-phonics programs are adopted because fidelity to the program typically trumps the actual goal of reading instruction, eager and autonomous readers. When a child is mandated to complete a phonics program, regardless of that child's needs, that time would have been much better spent with the child reading by choice; therefore, systematic-intensive phonics do in fact harm students when that is implemented as "all students must."

☐ *Feeding a false narrative blaming teachers and teacher educators both of whom are de-professionalized/powerless in accountability structures.* There are some dirty little secrets about education that discredit much of how media cover teaching and learning: As noted above, measurable teacher impact on student learning is quite small; teachers are mostly complying with mandates and not making instructional or assessment decisions; and teacher educators have very little impact on how teachers implement teaching once they are in the classroom and required to conform to the mandates linked to standards and high-stakes testing.

References

Bracey, G. (2006). *Reading educational research: How to avoid getting statistically snookered.* Portsmouth, NH: Heinemann.

DeWitt, P. (2019, June 9). 3 reasons I do not engage in Twitter debates. *Education Week.* Retrieved from http://blogs.edweek.org/edweek/finding_common_ground/2019/06/3_reasons_i_do_not_engage_in_twitter_debates.html

Krashen, S. (2017). *Does phonics deserve the credit for improvement in PIRLS?* Retrieved from http://www.sdkrashen.com/content/articles/2017_does_phonics_deserve_the_credit_for_improvement_in_pirls.pdf

CPSIA information can be obtained
at www.ICGtesting.com
Printed in the USA
LVHW081036240921
698620LV00001B/1